Insider Secrets of Internet Marketing

Strategies, Tips and Tricks for Online Business Success (Volumes 1-2)

MARK HENDRICKS

# # # # # # #

To get the audio MP3 recordings of this series,
you can visit this website:

http://hunteridge.com/2day

See more books by Mark Hendricks at:

http://amazon.com/author/markhendricks

And visit his main website at:

http://hunteridge.com

# # # # # # #

ISBN: 1482374498
ISBN-13: 978-1482374490

DEDICATION

To those who take action and persist until they succeed.

CONTENTS

How Do You Land That First Big JV When You Know You Have A Superior Product, But Your Best Potential JV Partners May See You As Direct Competition?

- Audio One Transcript -

Mark: Okay, welcome. I'm Mark Hendricks.

One of the things I want you to do this weekend is ask me a lot of questions because the more questions you ask, the more you are going to get out of my head.

I have been online doing business since about '94. Had my first domain; I had other Web sites but the first domain was in March of '96. That was www.Hunteridge.com

Prior to that I've been in business and marketing for almost 30 years now. So there is a lot of experience that I have, and to sit down and plan what I should teach somebody is difficult once you have a body of knowledge like that.

So the best way is for you to ask questions and when I give you answers, go ahead and let that develop more questions. Keep asking some questions and we will keep digging deeper into each topic. Okay?

So the first thing we can do, now I'll be standing up and sitting down, okay? I'm going to last longer if I sit down some.

How many of you, by show of hands, put some questions down? I think there were maybe 12 or so that did it.

Louis, you're up first, okay?

Louis said, "How do you land that first big JV when you know you have a superior product, but your best potential JV partners may see you as direct competition?"

That's a good question.

Joint ventures really start out as relationships that grow. Now, you'll want to take out a pen and paper, I guarantee it.

To grow relationships, and you are going to hear me talk a lot about relationships-those of you who are in Internet successes, and there will be a few of them around this weekend, I talk about this concept of know you, like you, trust you.

You have to work people through those three steps of: know who you are, begin to like you, and through that, they begin to trust you.

Because unless you take people through the three steps of know you, like you, and trust you they're not going to do business with you, they're not going to date you, they're not going to marry you, they're not going to do anything with you.

Every relationship is built on that, and it's the little, itty-bitty baby steps in a relationship, from the first time you meet somebody or become aware of somebody to where that blossoms into a relationship. Where it's a two way street, it's a give-and-take, and it's one of these things where we can live happily ever after.

So joint ventures. Your competitors, and I may need to ask you a little bit about it, and only share what you are willing to share. If it's something proprietary, hold back enough, but I may dig more, too. Okay?

With competitors, the first thing you have to do is know who they are-I'm assuming that you know who your major competitors are-and how they're approaching the marketplace and where you fit in with the marketplace.

You say you have a superior product and that can either be in your mind or that can be in the mind of the marketplace.

The way to develop relationships with your joint venture partners-can you give me a little idea about what the marketplace is, or just anything about the product?

Participant: Well, basically what I have done pretty much my whole life is, I found out at a very young age that I received my greatest joys when I was actually doing something that was helping to improve other people's lives.

So even though as life takes us in different paths; I have been primarily an IT consultant but I have always been very active in creating workshops and seminars and other sorts of self-development, or whatever you want to call those types of products. I've always done everything I could to make life easier for other people.

I've developed a series of products using the latest scientific technology, that will tap not just the conscious brain, but our unconscious self. I have learned a lot through my experiences as well as through my studies, that I know could be of a lot of help to people. I have gotten a lot of positive feedback from various products that I have either given away or sold.

But it seems that I am having trouble attracting the people who are willing to get involved, and help to take these concepts to another level.

So my products that I am focusing on now, really are combining the practical, "How to build a successful Internet home business," with these latest scientific discoveries in quantum physics and so forth, that show that we do in fact have the ability to influence, or I hate to use the word "create," more of our own reality than we are aware of.

Mark: How do you sell this concept at this point?

Participant: Well, I have a number of Web sites.

Mark: How do you deliver this product or service, at this point?

Participant: Everything is digital downloads.

Mark: Okay. So it's all digital downloads. Is it binaural beats? Does it do any of that kind of stuff, or what?

Participant: I have some of that but I haven't been marketing that over the Internet. I had marketed that via direct mail years ago.

Mark: Okay. Let me interject something. You may or may not have an interest in his marketplace, you may or may not sell or buy this kind of stuff, but what you will want to do is listen very carefully to the direction the conversation goes and translate this into your own marketplace.

That's really important all weekend long. Just because you don't think that it applies to you, believe me, it applies to you; the conversations that we will have.

Now the competitors of yours are speakers, scientists, big names in the industry?

Participant: Yeah, I mean there are a few entrepreneur-types who are now beginning to move into the marketplace, best known people being like Mark Anthony and Joe Vitale; those kinds of people.

For the most part, I get hundreds and hundreds of e-mails a day because of all the lists I am on, as well as through my own advertising efforts. For the most part, people are just interested in the practical, step-by-step, "what do I do?" kinds of things. Unfortunately, there's a lot material out there that just doesn't work, so you can waste a lot of time and energy.

Mark: Now, the step-by-step stuff, is it related to the mind stuff or the Web site stuff?

Participant: No, I am saying there aren't a whole lot of programs that combine the "build a home business using the technology of the Internet" while incorporating these success principles.

Mark: Why do you think that is?

Participant: I think it's just simply a lack of awareness by the general public, of this new knowledge that quantum physics has uncovered.

Mark: Okay.

One comment, whether I'm right or wrong, is that if you are marrying two concepts together, the marketplace can get confused. I mean, how many of us are this way? If you want to know something, you focus on that one thing and you kind of immerse yourself in that one thing.

So if somebody is having the biggest problem that they perceive, and it's their perception, their reality, is that, "I need to know how to make a Web site." Well, their reality is focused on that, and the other stuff of changing their mindset towards success is on the back burner.

Do you see what I mean?

Now, the thing that they may need the most is to have their mindset changed to where they're positive and they can see opportunities, and see that learning to design Web sites is the thing that they should spend their least time on. But their reality dictates that they see that they're focused on building Web sites.

So by combining the two, they look at a program, "Well here's how you do Web sites and you get a brain tune-up at the same time."

I am not talking lightly when I say a brain tune-up, okay?

They just see that as, "Well, I don't want that, I just want this," and they go look for something else.

A prospect is confused very, very quickly, if they don't understand the offer. So we need to make the offers very simple and very straightforward.

That's just a fact, no matter what marketplace you have. It's one of the problems we all have. We get immersed in the marketplace and we can see everything very clearly, because it's our reality.

I Don't Care How Somebody Thinks, I Want To Know How They Feel

It's one thing that hopefully you'll pick up this weekend; to be a good marketer you've got to flip yourself around to where you're on the market's side of the table.

You have to really, really understand how your prospects not only think, but feel about things.

That's where all the action is. It's in the feelings; it's not how they think.

I don't care how somebody thinks, I want to know how they feel.

I want to know what makes them tick. Not how they think, but what makes them tick, what makes them to take a step, an action. That's where all the stuff is.

That's how you get people to do things, is you understand their feelings when you come from their side of the table and understand their hopes and dreams and desires, their biggest doubts and fears and nightmares that they've got. If you can discuss those, then they see that you are one of them.

Now as far as joint venture partners, you are up against some pretty heavy hitters who've already got something going.

So maybe one thing you could do is to team up.

Are You An Expert, Or Not?

Well, here's another thing. Elsom Eldridge, how many of you know Elsom? A lot of you know the name. Elsom is one of the Internet Success System members, too. Elsom wrote a book, "How to Become the Obvious Expert in Any Marketplace in 90 Days or Less," or something like that.

He had a mentor when he was younger, and I can't recall the fellow's name. Yes, I can: Howard Shenson. Howard Shenson basically had Elsom write a book like in about a week or two. Howard told him, "Don't bother coming back until you've written the manuscript for your book."

Elsom didn't think he could do it, but he knew that he didn't need to bother coming back to this guy who knew how to make him an expert in the field until he wrote this book. So he wrote the book.

So my question is, do you have somebody of work that you can hand somebody that's an audio? Because all the people you are up against have what? Books and tapes. They're doing seminars, they're doing platform speeches, they're doing bootcamps and training and all this kind of stuff.

So you have to start some place where people can see what you're doing, okay?

The thing that each of you has to do is decide, if you haven't already done this, decide today that you, indeed, are an expert.

So everyone raise your hand who is an expert.

Good! We got past that hump. [Laughter]

Okay, I dub thee an expert!

Whatever you are into, you're the expert.

The interesting thing is, and I talked about this last weekend at our List Building Conference down in Orlando, I said that just by you declaring and having confidence that you're an expert, the majority of people who are interested in that subject will believe you.

That's just because you have enough gumption to stand up and say, "I'm the expert. Y'all listen to me!"

Now there's another portion that say, "Aah, I don't know. Let me hear you talk a little bit."

There's another portion that will say, "Prove it, because this guy says he's the expert."

Then they'll compare and shop.

But most people, if you have just enough stuff, they'll go along with it because people really do want to be led.

People want to be led.

People want to be led!

The ABCs Of Joint Ventures

Back to joint ventures. So they see you as a competitor. Rightly so, if you've got the new thing.

Now let's go back to developing relationships, though.

Anytime I approach anybody or think I'd like to do a joint venture with somebody, or if somebody approaches me with joint venture ideas, the best way to go about it is very, very slow.

It's not, "Hey, I've got this great product, it's the best thing in the marketplace. Your people will love it."

Well, if it happens to be that this person sells something along the same lines, you've got conflict rather than friendship, right?

So we've got to find out some way for you to get to know these people so they can what?

Know you, like you, and trust you.

So where do these people hang out?

Participant: Well, I communicate with them via e-mail, and I'm in the process of developing those relationships.

Mark: With these speakers who are already at some level?

Participant: Yeah, though I have not approached them with a joint venture idea.

Mark: Okay, so you're developing relationships now. Great.

Let me go through ABCs of joint ventures. I have a whole slideshow on this, but we're just going to talk through it.

The ABCs of joint ventures; you need to draw a picture on your notebook. Just take out one page and do this.

Right in the middle of the page you want to write the letter B. About 2-3" up you want to write the letter A, and about 2-3" down write the letter C.

Now down at the bottom of the page in the C area, I want you to write a whole bunch of Cs. Ten or more.

On the B-level, I want you to write oh, maybe six Bs; three to the left and three to the right.

On the top level, the A-level, I want you to write two more As; one to the left and one to the right of the A that you already have.

Now that B that's right there in the middle; put a circle around it, and that will be you.

Write the word "Me" on it.

This is your world.

You're not at the top, you're not at the bottom; always think of yourself as kind of in the middle

In your relationships, people coming along are the Cs, right?

The Bs are people that are at about your level.

Then there are going to be a few people who are further along than you, at the A-level.

Setting Up Joint Ventures With "A-Level" Players

Now, the tendency is when we starting looking to do joint ventures, where do we start looking for joint venture partners?

We always start looking at the As because they're further along, and we see that those people could help us the most, the quickest.

And you're absolutely right.

What's the only problem with thinking that way?

They're also the hardest to get to know sometimes because, guess what? They've already got their ABC network going.

They've gone through this process.

So you need to work at getting to know the As, by how? How can you get to know the people who are at the A-level?

Participant: Buy their products, go to their seminars.

Mark: Buy their products.

Go to their seminars.

Go to their seminars.

Go to their seminars.

Do I see the pens writing?

Go to their seminars.

Buying their products is good. That puts money into their pockets and you get to know what they're talking about.

But that's a one-way street, isn't it?

They have recorded their knowledge, their communication to people, either by studio or a live conference recording. They package that up and they sell that, and it's terrific for you to get the knowledge from it.

But the thing you want is the relationship, so you've got to set up situations to where you get to know the person.

Now, how can we get to know people? One is to go to seminars, but obviously that's not enough.

You actually have to talk to the person and meet the person, right?

Just like when you were little kids. I revert back to childhood in a lot of stuff that I'm going to teach you, because school screwed you up, to be blunt. [Laughter]

You know that little book, All I Really Need To Know I Learned In Kindergarten, or wherever it was? He was right! School really messed you up!

But think back, when you were four or five years old. How did you make friends?

You walked up and said, "Hey, do you want to be a friend?" And the kid either says yes or no. [Laughter]

It was really easy!

It was like, "Do you want to play? We'll have some fun."

It was nothing heavy. It was just that you wanted to be friends.

It was non-threatening. Then you let the relationship grow out of the laughter and the games that we played, right?

It's the same thing as an adult. Everybody gets a little too stuffy about this.

Just kind of relax and try to be friends.

The quickest way to get a friend, is to what?

Be a friend.

Now, what do friends do for each other? All kinds of stuff, right?

We're thoughtful, we are courteous, we try to be on the lookout. For somebody who's really a friend of ours, aren't we always on the lookout?

If you spot something, we'd say, "Oh, they would like that," or, "That would help with their situation," and you go ahead and get it for them.

You become like a servant. You are of service to those people, aren't you?

So, how could we do that with the As that we're trying to meet?

You get to their seminars; maybe they've got teleconferences, maybe they've got a training program. Just any way you possibly can to be part of their inner circle, the trusted people in their life.

You slowly get to know them that way, and you get to know them personally.

Not as the person on stage, not the persona.

Where do they have chinks in their armor, because we all do, right?

What aren't they good at?

Because joint ventures a lot of the time are about being able to bring different assets to the relationship that the other person doesn't have.

Now it may seem that they have it all together, but if you get to know them well enough, you'll spot some spots that you may be able to add something into it.

Now I just don't know your situation and what you are really good at.

See, the A-level, they've got their marketing machines built, so they've already pieced it together.

If you get to know them pretty well, you'll spot things. By the time they get to that level where you're seeing them at the top of their game, they basically show up and talk, right?

That's because they're the persona that drives the business, and they've got 3, 5, 10, 20, 100, 1,000 people working for them to make that happen, to where they can run up on the stage and do a 90-minute talk, or training for the weekend, and make it look easy.

But at some point in their life, how did they start off?

They were doing it themselves.

Participant: Hi. I do events in New York City with experts. Jeanette Cates came to speak on June 3rd.

Before, when I was planning it-she's a friend of mine now-and I said, "How do I get Alex Mandossian to send out the event to his list?"

She said one sentence. "Introduce him to Deepak."

Mark: There you go.

Yeah. You find out, "What do you want to know?" Or, "Who

wants to know who?" Then you put the thing together and all of a sudden you're friend. Right.

So that's a clue.

Participant: Hi. I'm Katie from Columbia, Maryland. From what I have noticed on this A-list, you're talking about $2,000-$3,000 to go to a seminar. So how do you get to know these people when you don't have $2,000-$3,000?

Mark: Well, that would be any teleseminars that they do that are close.

In the scheme of things, a lot of times they'll have a book that cost $20 and the audios are a little higher, and the videos are a little higher. Then the teleseminar training, and now you have the weekend things, and all that kind of stuff. So it's a pyramid of piling money, is what it is.

Most models are built that way in the infomercial business. So you just have to plug in wherever you can.

Now, the other way you can go, if you are a raving fan of theirs, do they have an affiliate program?

Could you help sell their stuff? If you want to make a friend really quick, start selling their stuff.

Number one, you get their attention and two, you can finance your way to their seminars.

Or even better, you might even get invited as a bonus, right?

You say, "You know, I have sold a bunch of your product; I just wonder if you had a situation where I could come out and come to your seminar, and maybe work for the weekend. Help at the welcome table?"

I mean, there are a lot of seminars that I go to where there will be a person or two at the front of it. They're doing the check-in kind of thing and kind of go for this and go for that, and all that kind of stuff, to get to know and be on the inside of the situation.

So whatever you can do to get close.

There's a fellow that may come tomorrow, or this afternoon. I can't remember when he said he might drop by. He's gotten really good at setting up joint ventures.

He usually does joint ventures with people who are outside of his market niche. His products sells well in a lot of different market niches, but he has developed a whole system to where he develops a joint venture relationship by mail. Like mailing crazy stuff in the mail to them, to get their attention with a letter and a copy of his product.

It lets people know who else he has done joint ventures with, what kind of response, and he has done terrifically well.

He's one of my first apprentices from about three years ago, and he's just doing terrific now.

So that's one way.

Then if you've got something to help develop a relationship; a FedEx package, he has done baby bottles. He puts the mailing address and postage on a baby bottle and sends the baby bottle through the mail.

In your mail you get this baby bottle with a message stuck inside; you know, the letter.

That's going to get the attention.

Now that's just part of the thing, is getting the attention. You actually have to have an offer to get the relationship going again.

Lou, anything that I have said helped? Or let's go deeper?

Participant: Well, everything that you've said I agree with wholeheartedly, and I'm in the process of putting more effort into those activities.

No More Excuses, Just Go Do It

Mark: Have you gone to the seminars where these guys are?

Participant: Well, that's been one of my problems, is I have very limited time because of all the activities that I'm involved with, besides doing a full-time consulting job.

So although I have spent tens of thousands of dollars investing in courses and teleseminars and so forth, I haven't had the opportunity to fit into my schedule or price range some of the really big events that I would like to attend.

Mark: Okay. This weekend you'll pull out your date book. I'm going to show you my brilliance here, this is how easy it is, folks.

You're going to schedule, you're going to find one and you're going to schedule it in. You are going to put everything else around that.

Because you've just told me that your main goal is to do this, right?

Participant: Yeah, I believe that I have...

Mark: No excuses. I'm hearing excuses started to come out. Can you hear that?

Participant: No, no. It's not an excuse. I was just going to say that I believe that I do have products already created and products that I am in the process of developing that I think will be attractive to potential joint venture partners.

So I'm going to do everything that I can to work my way to the point where I can develop the relationships to the level that they need to be.

Mark: Okay, this weekend, like in tomorrow. You'll be here tomorrow, right? Tomorrow you're going to tell everybody which conference you're going to, and when it is.

All right? We're not letting you off the hook.

All of these people, look around at these smiling faces. These are your friends!

Participant: Fair enough!

Mark: Okay. It can be three months from now, or a year. I don't care when it is, but you're going to have it in your date book. Everything else gets scheduled around that.

Could I do that to everybody?

Yeah.

Would everybody like to do that?

I don't care. Whoever it is that you'd really love to go hear speak, this weekend see if you can do some research to figure out when is the next time they're going to do it.

Or if you can't swing it the very next time, six months later or a year later.

I don't care when it is, but put it down and stick it up on your mirror and do all those positive things that everybody teaches you to do.

Except for the one thing that you don't do well is to take the action to do it!

Right? Am I right?

Okay, this is the difference in me. I am very, very focused.

If I decide to do something, I am tenacious. I am persistent.

I never, ever give up. I will keep working on things.

People tell me, "You are nuts!"

I say, "You're right!"

[Laughter]

But I am tenacious that way.

So focus, focus, focus!

Some people call it the zone. You just get so focused that everything else goes away.

You just work on that, and you have that laser beam focus on getting what it is and where you want to be.

Just keep working on that and chiseling away and chiseling away and chiseling away.

You know that old story about the old sculptor? "How do you make this beautiful statue?"

He says, "It's easy. I just chip away everything that doesn't look like the final product."

[Laughter]

That's the kind of process.

It's like the old gold prospector.

People asked him, "How do you find so much gold?"

"I throw away all the other stuff, and then I've got gold."

That's kind of what you've got to do as far as this focus kind of stuff goes.

I still don't feel like I've helped you out that much, though.

Participant: As an example, as I was leaving my apartment in Brooklyn Heights yesterday, I've got mail. It was from Hay House and it was this big, huge seminar in October, with people like, Wayne Dyer and 20 other great people like him and I said, "Wow!"

But then there's air fare, conference fare, and everything; the cost of everything. The first thing that came to my mind was, "I am going to call and see if I can volunteer." That's where I usually find it.

Mark: Yeah, if you keep asking all those speakers, too. If there are that many speakers, how many offices can you call and say, "Hey, do you need some help with just picking up junk and moving it around?"

There has to be some way to be able to weasel in, somehow.

What Is It That People Want And Will Pay Money For

Let me give you another thing to write down.

You've all heard about other people's money; using other people's money.

You can use other people's money to get anything that you want, and that's one of things that I do. If there's something that my family or I want, I'll just say, "Okay, what can I sell that other people would give me their money for?"

Because that's all we're doing, and its very, very simple.

If you get your mind tweaked this way, it's like money becomes very, very easy. But you have to understand your marketplace where you are working.

What is it that people want and will pay money for? If you can quickly get that out to them, you'll be trading their money for whatever product that you can sell them.

It doesn't have to be your product, right? It can be someone else's product.

That's the best of all the possible worlds. You get other people's money by selling them somebody else's product, and you didn't have to take the time to develop the product.

So if you want to take a trip someplace and it costs X thousands of dollars, then think, "What can I sell that is going to bring in whatever thousands of dollars, so that I can do what I want to do?"

I give people what they want to do and I get the money so that I can do what I want to do.

That makes the world go around.

And the cool thing is, if you sell enough of what they want and you don't spend it all, your net worth keeps going up. Then the whole thing becomes more of a game, which is where you want to be, because it's a lot of fun.

Then you can test and tweak and try things, and the amazing thing is the things you never thought would work, because you're using your logical brain, work. That's because they tap into the emotional situation of the marketplace.

More On Getting To Know People And Joint Ventures

Let's go back to getting to know people and joint ventures.

So, one of the best things you can do is to find out is what that person is into, and it's usually not business. Everybody thinks in business terms, but why do people do business?

Number one, it can be fun, it can be a challenge; but it's usually because of the rewards that business gives us.

Most of the time people think of business as money first, right? It usually starts there.

The second thing that comes into it is power; influence.

Now we're getting the ego thing into it.

But after the money, power and influence, what do people cherish most above those things?

It's time, right?

So how can you be a person, if somebody already has the money and power and influence thing going, how can you help them get more time? It's because you're willing to commit your energy; whether it be time, or money, or effort, to put them in that position where they do have more time.

It's your job to figure out how you fit into their situation, so that you have the opportunity to help them in that manner.

Now that's a puzzle, and I don't have an answer for you there, because you have to get to know the person that well, to be able to spot that situation.

It happens all the time. People approach me to do joint ventures, "I've got this product. Would you send it to your list, I will pay you X. "

I get those all the time. What's unique about it? What makes you think that the people that know, like, and trust me, would be interested in it? What makes you think that, here, you're a person that I've never heard of, I have no clue who you are, is approaching me with that.

That doesn't bother me so much, because new relationships start that way. I'm easier than the most, because I know how the thing starts and that doesn't put me off.

However, for somebody to do that out of the blue, it's like seeing a woman for the first time and saying, "Do you want to kiss?"

I guess sometimes it would work out, but other times you might get slugged!

Or the relationship at least is over before it had a chance to blossom at all.

So you've got to find a way, Lou, to start the relationship, to know.

Participant: Well, I appreciate all of your comments, and I think what they've done for me, mostly, is just to confirm that I am doing what I need to do.

Mark: Okay. But we need to come out with something more unique for you. That's what I'm after here. Without knowing exactly what you're doing and how you're doing it, it's kind of hard to drill down.

Participant: I can bring some materials in tomorrow, just to give you an idea.

Mark: Also, one of the thoughts that I had was, have you gotten warmed up to somebody in the marketplace? I mean, to where they're noticing you, at least?

Participant: Yeah, I've made some connections, but not with any of the big hitters yet.

Mark: Now let me ask you another question, and here's something you've got to look at real close, folks. The people that you are trying to joint venture with, look and see if they're already doing joint ventures.

If they're not doing joint ventures, you may be banging your head against the wall.

If they're the kind of person who has their own empire and, "Anything that's not invented here is not being presented to the public or their customer base," if that's the situation you're going to have a hard time getting in.

That's because it's just not in their mentality, at this point in time. The biggest problem that you have is educating them as to why they should be interested in joint ventures. That education is very expensive and time-consuming.

You'd prefer to spot somebody who has already snapped to the idea of joint ventures and is willing to promote other people's products.

Another thing, too; look at the speakers.

Now I'm giving you good stuff, it's starting to roll, okay? I can feel it; here it comes.

For instance, when you go to the seminars, if Mr. and Mrs. Big are putting up a seminar for a three-day weekend, do they also have other speakers there? Or is it just them the whole weekend?

If it's just them the whole weekend doing training, chances are, joint ventures may not be in their life. If it's where they're talking half the time and they have five or six other people talking, and the stuff is getting sold in the back of the room and the whole business, then there are some deals going on.

So this is one of the things that I'll tell you.

Write this down.

Life leaves clues. You've got to be a good detective.

Success leaves clues.

If the whole weekend, and I don't mean speakers within their organization, I mean speakers who are at their level or the next level of up-and-comers. Are they helping pull people up through the ranks? If that's the case, those are the ones you want to go after.

The ones where it's just their show; they've got their hirelings that they're grooming themselves and they are part of the organization, it's probably going to be hard for you to break into that situation.

Would you agree?

Can you spot that in your market, where there are those two different types?

Participant: Oh, absolutely.

Mark: So there are some like that? Then I would, at this stage of the game, if it's a single system where it's just a big shot, I would put them way back on your list of trying to deal with, and go for the ones who do provide opportunities.

The other thing, too, and this goes back to ABCs. You want to be the kind of person who helps people up.

We all talk about being nice and helpful, but I mean really helping people up. There are a couple of reasons that you want to do this.

One is that it's a good thing to do. You're being a friend, therefore you will make a friend. Number two, a lot of those people who are at the level below you are going to make it, with or without you. You need to spot those up-and-comers who you can help.

Now understand, they will be a winner with or without you, so you might as well help them, right?

Now, will those people always help you? No.

Will they sometimes forget that you help them? Yes, but I guarantee that you will learn a lot from helping them. Some of the stuff that they know, and the reason why they're moving up quickly, you can pick up stuff from them, too.

It's always a two-way street.

I always love spotting people who are on their way up. Those are the kind of people that I like to say, "Here, grab my hand. Let's go," and, "What do you know that I don't know?" Because there's always something that somebody knows that I don't know. I'm going to learn as much as I can from everybody.

Those people who don't remember that you helped, don't worry about it.

A Little Story To Remember: There Are 360 Degrees In A Circle

There's something I learned, oh, my goodness, that many years ago, nearly 20 years ago, was a circle has 360° in it. I mean, I knew it prior to that, but it didn't snap to what I am about to tell you.

If I help people in this direction, like Lou, here; all of us, if we help somebody, we tend to think that Lou should be helping me back, right? Reciprocity.

What happens if Lou doesn't do that? It's human nature to go, "Well, I did that favor for Lou and that rascal, he didn't help me back."

But what am I blind to? That's only one degree of the circle, isn't it? What about the other 359° of life happening around me?

All those other degrees are always flowing to you, aren't they, in all kinds of different ways that unless you're tuned into them, you miss them completely. And you're not grateful for all the blessings that you have.

So I'm going to tell you, you've got to just keep pumping good out, one degree at a time, as much as you can, and somehow it's going to come back from that direction. But I guarantee that the other 359° of circle is where the action is.

If that's getting a little too spiritual for you, so be it; because that's where it flows from.

What did you get out of this, Lou?

Participant: Well again, it's all great information, and it's confirmation that I'm doing what I should be doing. I guess I just want it to happen a little faster, that's all.

Mark: What's the one thing you need to be doing more of?

Participant: I have to focus more on getting my products and services out there, as opposed to developing products and services. I've been shifting my attention in that direction in order to do that.

So, I'm increasing the contact that I have with others, whether they are customers or people that I have purchased products from, or potential joint venture partners or not, which is one of the reasons I am here today.

Setting Up Joint Ventures With "B-Level" Players

Mark: Let's go to another level now. We've just been talking about the A-level, haven't we? What about the B-level? These are the people at about your same level, who have the same kind of problems that you do.

Have you spotted those in your marketplace?

Now we've have got him, huh?

[Laughter]

I'm kidding you a little bit. Thanks for being a good sport!

The B-level is where you'll probably get a lot of your action, because these are the ones who are hungry and trying to get to the A-level. Not all of them are going to make it. However, you can have a very, very nice level of living at whatever level you choose, right?

It's going to be easier to get to know those people. Their conferences, their marketing systems, their products may not be as expensive, and it may be that they're more welcome to the idea of joint ventures and helping.

They don't have the turf to defend.

The A-level people have already claimed their stake. Do you understand that? They've got the relationships and they're hand-in-hand already. To get them to break hands and let a new person in and join hand-to-hands is tougher than at the B-level.

The B-level is like, "Okay, let's all huddle up and take care of each other," because guess what? That's how A happened. They had the

B ranks and they huddled up, and they all got to move up to another level.

Now, what makes you think you can't do that?

Still work on your A relationships.

Why is that important?

See, if you develop your own network of ABC, and you do have the opportunity, and once again, opportunity is when what happens?

You get your chance when your preparation meets the opportunity. That's what I'm trying to say.

That could be your successful moment, your moment in time, when you finally do get to talk to A and get their attention. You get to speak with them a little bit and all of a sudden they discover you've developed your whole network of people. Why is that valuable?

Because they make one connection with you, and what do they get out of this? They get the whole circle. They get everything that you built because of the relationship with you. Now can you see where you just added value to the relationship?

Stop focusing on A so much, and start focusing on Bs and Cs, and being helpful to Bs and Cs that know you, like you, and trust you.

One day you will have an opportunity to hook up with an A, and you will then say, "I've got all these people who know, like, and trust me. When I make a recommendation that they do something, they will do it."

How viable is that to an A? Terrific!

Now Bs. Where do we find Bs? They may be doing their own

programs, their own conferences, selling their own products. Where else might you find them?

Look around at somebody else's seminar or workshop.

Participant: Also through newsletters.

Mark: Through newsletters; all these forms of communication that we have.

Participant: I think meeting Bs is very easy in private membership forums. I'm a part of a couple of them, and that's really where I think a lot of people tend to be more willing to share authentically what they're struggling with. They're open to private messaging and talking back and forth, and sharing on the same level. I have found, in terms of developing my own network with folks that I would say are on the B-level, would be very much so in the private forums.

Also, as far as the A-level, the forum moderators are those that are the "coaches." Those folks, many of them are very well established in whatever that area is. That can be sort of your first in into an A, that I have seen.

Mark: Okay, good advice.

Now let's talk about forums for a second. There are a lot of negative people hanging around the forums. Don't waste your time with those people.

One of the things that I spend zero time on, is if anybody wants to make negative comments, I just don't even respond. It's just not worth it. That little thread goes away or some other negative people will grab onto it and take their time doing it.

Now that's kind of an Internet thing, but it's the same thing in a live situation.

You know as well as I, you get to some places and somebody's sour grapes because of somebody else's success.

How much time do you want to hang around with those people? You don't.

You want to hang around with winners. Whether they are As, Bs or Cs, your job is to find winners and associate yourself with winners.

Where else can we find Bs?

Participant: Hi, Marty Stride. I just want to say that the way I found some Bs and developed a good relationship with an A is to get involved in some type of a long-term training program. I was in one with Alan Bechtold, but Mark's Internet Success System, any type like that.

You're involved for a really long time and you get to know the other members really well. I've developed five or six friends who are at my level in marketing, and we communicate; phone calls and e-mails. Potential JV partners as we develop are right there.

The A-level, you get to know that person really well. They become a friend for life, and if I need to do a JV with that A person, I feel fairly confident that I'm not going to have any trouble.

Mark: Right. At least you can easily approach the person. They may not have the time to do it but they will be very helpful to you, and help you put the program together. Absolutely.

Participant: Right. They need to protect their integrity with their list.

Mark: Absolutely.

The great thing about what Marty just talked about, and thanks for bringing that up, is if you do these training programs or apprenticeship programs, like with Alan or me or whoever you warm up to. It doesn't really matter. What I suggest you do is look for somebody who is willing to do a two-way street.

You don't want to get into relationships that are only going to be one-way streets. Do you know what I mean? It's always going to be AB-AB. You'd like to feel that at some point you have the chance of becoming more equal. I'm looking for that in all the relationships that I do.

My thing, and it's up there just to fill up the screen, but there are lots of joint ventures that have come out of the ISS program. Some with me, some the members did with themselves, like Marty was saying with Alan's thing. Alan's got a great program.

So that's some good advice.

Setting Up Joint Ventures With "C-Level" Players

How about C-level? How can you spot up-and-comers?

Have you ever seen new products coming out of nowhere that's like, "Wow! Where did that come from? Great idea!"

Do you know why they come up like that? It's like Lou's got all these ideas popping out of his head.

The superstars in the industry are out there yakking, resting on what they have already done. They're always coming up with new products. Have you noticed, how many times can a superstar say the same thing?

Yeah, a lot of times it's just a repackaged, right? I mean, it's the same stuff they have always been saying, and why is that?

Once they become the persona, I mean, they built their whole thing on that and that's their mindset, too. I mean, how hard is it to change how they think and feel about life?

Each one of the people who's a leader in a field like that has a certain twist on life, that a certain portion of society, the population, is attracted to.

Do you notice that there's a lot of room at the top? That's because everybody sees life a little bit different, and we all get attracted to a different personality.

That's okay.

One of the things that you will discover, it's okay that the whole world doesn't love you. You'll become comfortable with that.

Some people will go through Mark's training program and other people will go through Alan's training program. They're both good. Alan's a good guy; I'm a good guy. It's just that for whatever reason, people are attracted to different things, and you get comfortable with that. It's not jealousy at that point. Alan and I frequently do things together.

Participant: You had asked a little while ago, how do you find Cs? I learned something, I read somewhere recently where one technique was to go to ClickBank and they have that affiliate program with all the products. They're weighted by how good they are. The top ones are at the top, but go down the list of the new ones that have just come out that are at the bottom, and there might be nuggets of gold in there. There might be some great new products that just started, and that may be one way of finding the Cs.

Mark: If you remind me, I'll show you my software that I developed, to be able to do that stuff really quick, because I do the same thing. I'll go through there, and you've got all the top ones, and I can filter all the top sellers right now. I also like to go down in there, and if I'm working on a particular market niche, I go down and find stuff that nobody has ever heard of. I go looking around and spotting stuff and see if I can develop a relationship with that person and maybe work a special deal, or any kind of leverage I've got with the person, to do something special.

Those things nobody knows about, and here's something completely fresh to throw at the marketplace. I've done that with a couple of people and it has made their whole business. They were just nowhere, and all of a sudden, bam! I hit it and it took off, and it gave them credibility in the marketplace to where they could talk to other people.

The 12 Days Of Christmas Cross-Promotion Strategy

Some of you know me and that "12 Days of Christmas" thing that I've done for the last few years, which is like the first one of these big giveaways.

Chris Lockwood, who is an ISS member, we were talking last week at the List Building Conference that I did. Chris interviewed me on that, and he says, "Since you're the guy who came up with this giveaway stuff, I thought maybe it would be good to interview you about it, Mark."

[Laughter]

I didn't even think about that, and I told him that I dreamed that whole thing up on December 1st, three years ago, at five o'clock in the morning. People always thought that I must have prepared that for months and months and months that first time, which was 2003.

December 1, 2003, I literally woke up and my eyes opened and I said, "What am I going to do this month, because everybody is buying presents and spending money for family, friends, grandparents, spouses, kids, you name it. What do they want to hear from me?"

I thought, "Okay, why don't I do some kind of a promotion, a freebie thing?"

So I thought, "Hmm, Christmas. The 12 Days of Christmas is a song."

This is the process that went through my head.

So I sent an e-mail to five people and said, "Here's what I want to do. Do you want to do it with me?" Three of them wrote back.

So the first day of Christmas was me, one gift.

I knew I wanted to end it right before Christmas, so I had to do it every other day. The good news was that brought me two days, right?

Time!

[Laughter]

So I was the first day, it got the thing going, just out to my list. Then, on December 3, here were the next two. Then I had a one more. Remember I had three people, so I already had the third day of Christmas, December 5, I had one of three lined up. So you see, this thing literally snowballed over that time period.

It went on and on and on, until that first year there were 78 people involved in that gift thing. Then the second year had a couple of little changes and the third year had a couple of little changes.

So I'm still having to one-up all these other people who imitate that whole thing. I'm trying to think of what the big one-up is going to be this year. I haven't figured it out yet, but something will come up.

That's how it all started, and it just happened to catch on. I've got my thoughts as to why it does better than the other ones, which I won't share.

Participant: My thought is that you are such a giver that the universe gives you back so much.

Mark: Well, you know I will share that with you, and yeah, I think that's true. An interesting thing that I learned during those three years of doing that, and I would write to the contributors frequently about this.

I said, "I noticed in the statistics of how many people were being sent by contributor, when they would continually market the program, the giveaway thing to their list. I have statistics showing me where all the traffic is coming from, and I also have statistics on how many people the program sent to their site. Invariably, the people who sent more traffic to this site got more people going to their site."

Some people say, "You stacked it and you played favorites."

No, and that's what really caught my attention, is that the people who gave the most received the most. I would write to people, and the ones who get it would practice it and they would get more, and the ones that didn't, they just, for some reason the universe wouldn't reward them.

Participant: That leads me to another question similar to this, dealing with building your list. I know a lot of these giveaway programs and giveaway books, et cetera, are targeted to develop your list of folks that you can develop a relationship with long term.

How do you deal with the fact that many people are joining or linking up with you, in terms of a subscriber base, because they're "freebie seekers"? They're really just in it for what you can give to them and they have no inclination to spend money and, of course, ultimately bring revenue to you. How do you make those distinctions in terms of the quality of your list?

Mark: Okay, great question.

You have to know that going in, that a lot of people are just going to do the freebie thing. So don't get your hopes up. Just because you've got lot of people on your list, a lot of them are freebie-seekers.

However, that's usually the first step in the relationship. The big mistake that people make when they do these giveaways is that they start slamming these people with offers to buy stuff right off the beginning.

Therefore people think, "I've got my freebie; now they're hitting me up for money, I'm out of here," instead of building relationship over time.

That's the thing that I insisted, like that first year, because I told people, "If you try to sell something to these people in December, I cut you out." I was that tough about it.

I don't know about most of these giveaways, but I have real stern rules of what I'm looking for. I look at every product that gets contributed.

Now a couple, two or three, somehow sneak by me every year it seems, even though I go through this process. Or they switch things on me, and what they said they're going to give away, they give away something else.

People write to me and say, "Hey this person is not playing the way they're supposed to be," and I then check into it and I usually give them 24 hours to fix it or they're out.

Most of the time a person will fix it half-and-half. The other times I get some third-grade kind of attitude like, "What do you mean? What did I do?"

So I just write back and say, "Come on. Fix the problem."

Or people are signing up and they're not getting the gift and all this kind of stuff, and they come back with an excuse. I just say, "Look, you have 24 hours to fix it or forget it."

I don't put up with that because if we have problems like that it tarnishes the whole project; it really affects everybody.

The first year it was, "Don't hit people with offers, don't slam them, because people won't come in the front door of the giveaway if all they're doing is getting a freebie so you can try to sell something, bam!"

That was kind of it the second year. In the third year I started allowing like one-time offers, but I would still say, "I want to see what your freebie is and I want to see what your one-time offer is."

Most these things, they don't care. Whatever you want to contribute or sell, go ahead.

But I'm really concerned about the quality and how people are being treated because if they're not being treated well they won't tell other people what a great deal this is to get all these terrific things.

Like Bob mentioned, "I can't believe the quality of stuff that I got," and he was just involved this last year. That's the reason why, is I really try to get stuff that people are selling for the rest of the year, not just something that they grabbed off of some resale-rights shelf someplace.

That's the other thing; if I see somebody wanting to contribute something that I've seen floating around, I just tell him, "Come on, we've got to come up with something better than that."

That's how I differentiate it, I guess. That may be enough to help differentiate. I don't know.

MARK HENDRICKS

How To Make Money From Your List

Now how to-back to your question, Dana. That really all comes back into list building and learning how to profit from the list.

It's being able to write; if you publish weekly, which is the minimum that I would suggest you do. Anyone who knows me knows that I publish any time I feel like it, if there's something worthwhile. It's just my view on it.

I see a lot of stuff and people on my list depend on me to let them know when something is happening. If people don't like it, there is always a link down at the bottom where they can get off.

So I don't concern myself with that too much, but once a week assume that people really do want to hear from you. If you're an advocate for your marketplace, if you want to write that down, it's really important.

If you want to be an advocate for your marketplace, be on the lookout for stuff. Go out and be the pioneer; find things and report back to them.

Remember, because who's an expert?

Yeah, I am an expert, right? Remember?

The expert is the one out there on the front lines, seeing what's going on and telling everybody else all about it.

Some of the things you might write in it, most people call that a newsletter; right? You need to look at it as a personal letter with news. You want to write a personal letter that has news in it, just like you are writing to a family member or a best pal.

That's the feel.

That could be something new that you found out.

My gosh, it could be a conference you went to in Baltimore, couldn't it?

If you have a list of people you write to on a periodic basis, how many of them are here today? Right? Wouldn't this be a good thing to report back on? Would that position you as an expert, as somebody who is doing something?

A lot of times, you will see me, if I go speak at a conference; every time that I speak at a conference I put out an e-mail from that conference. It says something about who I met, who I saw, what I was impressed with, and a list of people who came up and shook hands and we smiled, right?

I did this about three or four weeks ago in Orlando.

Now what does that do? It lets you know that I have been someplace, it also tells you who I am hanging around with, and the third thing it does is I just promoted those other people, right? There were As, and there were Bs, and there were Cs.

So I gave. Some of those people will give back, some won't. It doesn't matter.

You just have to start getting the ball rolling; you've just got to keep your ball going.

Just keep paddling. [Laughter]

That's what I tell my wife. I said, "I'm really not trying to steer, I learned that I have just got to paddle. The steering always hits the rocks. That's because I don't know where the rocks are, so I just paddle."

Have you ever tried that? Stop trying to steer your boat! Just paddle.

I'm seeing a lot of smiles.

You ever notice that? You end up on a rock when you try and try, and you crash.

Try for awhile. Just paddle.

Participant: Just to add what you said about writing in your newsletter, an event like this can actually give you enough material to do three or four issues. It's very helpful.

Mark: Oh, easily. Yeah.

The other things that you can talk about; you may find some freebies. If people like freebies once, guess what? They will like them twice, believe me.

Everybody likes a freebie, and especially a freebie that you had to scratch for, or that you came up with yourself that nobody else has got.

Write this down, okay?

Unique.

You've got to be unique, you've got to find your way.

Just like Lou's situation, he's kind of banging heads with the people who already are at a certain level, and he is trying to aspire to rise to that level, to play in that league.

You've got to be you.

Participant: Yeah, I just want to ask you a question relating to this. In the newsletter that I do publish, I do give away in every issue, freebies that are good quality. I was wondering, because it has been suggested to me that perhaps part of my problem is that my list of readers has gotten used to getting good material free from me, that's one of the reasons they're not buying.

Mark: I would suggest that you mix it up so that people don't know every time. If you're doing it by e-mail, this will get people to always open your e-mails because they don't know what's inside. Like a box of Cracker Jacks; you know that there's something in there, but you're not sure what. So you're going to open it up to look, at least.

It becomes a little game of, "What could it be this time?" Because you never know. I would try some of that.

What Is Better Than Content?

The other thing that you want to do, and I talked about this at length at list building things and copywriting things.

Write this down.

You've heard of content. Content is king, right?

Write that down.

Then on top of that, write BS. Just write over the top of "Content is king" with big letters, "BS."

The next thing that you will hear is this thing about relevant content; and take your pen again and write "BS."

The thing that I would suggest you do is to get good at what I call "actionable content," and this is not BS.

This is what your content needs to be.

Content meaning the communication that you're doing with a person; whether it be written or audio or video, or whatever it is.

Actionable content is communication that leads somebody else to an action.

It's not good enough just to throw content up on the page. It's not good enough that the content is relevant to what they're looking for. What you're doing as a marketer is leading the way.

When you are providing whatever the content is, you've got to provide-here it is, circle it-always be providing the next step.

Always be providing the next step.

Let me give you a prime example. Is there anything in this room that would hint for you what the next step might be?

Marty spotted it.

Is it subtle?

Actually, I was just trying to fill the screen with something, and this works.

Is this weekend actionable content, as you see it now?

Okay, good. Everybody understands, right?

Now the interesting thing is, I'm not afraid to tell you exactly what I do. Most speakers won't tell you. As I'm going, I can detail exactly what's happening to you psychologically, and reveal all the stuff that I am able to do to you, psychologically.

Interestingly, it doesn't matter because it's still going to work on you at a lower level. That's what's so fascinating about this stuff.

We'll probably talk this after awhile. There are six psychological triggers, that if you can learn to do these, and I will go through them with you later on some time this weekend sometime, I'm sure.

They're really, really important for you to know and to master.

The other things that you can do in a newsletter; we talked about freebies, actionable content.

How about guest articles, referrals to others?

Here's another idea, Lou. How about joint venture partners; this is going to work well on As, Bs, and Cs. It doesn't really matter.

Their product line; you get in contact with them and you say, "I have a whole bunch of readers who I publish to on a weekly basis," or whatever it is, and we can spend a few minutes talking about this, "and I'm always looking for other products that they may be interested in. Would you happen to have an affiliate program for your product line?"

Most of them probably will, or you could work out something, I'm sure.

Invite Possible Joint Venture Partners To Be Interviewed By You On A Teleseminar

The other thing you would want to do, if at all possible, is set up a teleseminar situation where they're your guest, and you are going to position yourself as the interviewer and have them on as a guest. You are going to ask them about their body of work.

Don't ask the same ten questions to everybody. I don't know how many, there is a lot of this e-books and stuff going around and they send out the same ten questions to everybody. Everybody fills in the blank and sends them back and you've got this e-book thing.

When I see those I just don't want to participate, because I know the person hasn't really learned anything about me. They just have their preconceived idea of these ten questions that everybody wants to know, which is really boring to me.

If I am doing a situation where I want to interview somebody, I'll get a copy of their book, I'll look at their Web pages and sales letters and pull out what this person is all about. That becomes my 10-20 questions.

The other thing that I want to do to is have this person I'm interviewing provide me with 10-20 questions that they want me to ask.

Get it?

I want to come up with my own questions but I also want them to provide me with questions. If they match up, terrific. If I've got some questions that aren't on there, that's good, too.

Right?

Because what am I? I'm an advocate for my marketplace, and the things that I like to ask people are all the questions that people should be asking them the next level down. Not the superficial stuff that everybody talks about. I really want to get into the nitty-gritty with them.

Now, am I going to surprise them with those questions with everybody listening and the tape player recording the thing? No. I'm going to give them the list of questions and I'm going to give them, in a logical sequence, how this phone call is going to unwind.

By doing that little bit of preparation, that teleconference will go really, really smoothly. It will always have direction, and it won't be wandering all over the place.

And what can I do? This now becomes what? Content? Relevant content? Or does it become actionable content?

See, I'm leading the way and I know where this call wants to go.

There has to be some next step.

There is always the next step.

So you can have that in your newsletter, the invitation to those kinds of things. Or maybe you did a private teleconference where it was just you and one other person. You didn't invite anybody to listen to it; it's just a telephone call. You got somebody on there and you got going and talking and said, "Can I report this? I've got some people that would love to hear it." Now you have some more actionable content that introduces people to somebody that you know.

How To Be Quickly Recognized As An Expert

Now, let's talk about you being an expert again. The big, big expert happens if you can become an expert by association. Does that happen? Right, because if you've got enough stuff to be able to interview experts, where does that position you? As an expert, right? That's your circle that you hang out with.

So one of the quickest ways to become a recognized expert is to what? Interview experts.

A lot of people have gotten expert status because of that one thing.

What else could you do in the newsletter?

Reviews? Product reviews? Sometimes tied to an affiliate link and sometimes not. Wouldn't that be nice?

Now if you're not going to tie it to an affiliate link, it might be a situation where you could do a cross-promotion with somebody. That might help you a little bit.

The A players may not want to do this; the B players could be very interested in this. That's where you cross-promote to your list.

Marty talked about cross-promoting to his list. Wouldn't somebody else subscribe to somebody else's letter, and wouldn't some of those people subscribe to yours? And the answer is, "Absolutely, yes."

But what happens over time? Remember, people gravitate to people that they know, like, and trust the best. Some of them from their list will probably gravitate my way and guess what's going to happen? Some of them from my list are going to gravitate their way.

They should have been there to begin with, right?

So are you still being of service to those people? Yeah. You helped them to get where they should have been. If I'm not making sense, we need to find somebody who makes sense to you, and that's the best thing that I could do.

By doing so, my relationship with that person, the joint venture partner or whoever I recommended they go talk with, that solidifies my relationship with that person. Therefore I have a better chance of reciprocity.

What else could we do in a newsletter?

Preview. Tell them what's coming up.

Curiosity. If you're planning these things a few weeks in advance, or if you know it's coming up, you can create curiosity. Not telling what it is, but just tease. "News at eleven." Has anybody ever heard that?

Now they do it, they lead you right up to commercial break and then it's like, "Okay, we'll let you know right after the commercial break."

It used to be at the six o'clock news at night, they would tease us hours later. Now it's like they do it in two minute chunks. "We'll tell you when we get back from the commercial break."

How about reminding people of things? In your current newsletter, could you remind people about what you talked about a week ago, two weeks ago?

That maybe you overlooked this, or that you've gotten some good feedback from other people?

What else can you do?

I'll tell you one of the greatest secrets and you need to write this down.

What's the easiest way to find out what people want to know, do, or buy, or have done?

Participant: Ask them!

Mark: www.YouAskThem.com YouAskThem.com.

And I'm telling you, since developing that software; see, I used to send out little surveys just by e-mail. I'd say, "If you could do me a favor, let me know what you think about this. What are you looking to do?"

I mean thousands of people would write back, and the feedback that you get just by asking people what they think, how they feel about things, is phenomenal.

It gets you right into your marketplace, and the most amazing thing is it builds a relationship that you have with them, because most people don't ask people what they want.

MARK HENDRICKS

Should You Bribe People To Give You Feedback?

Participant: Quick question on that note, Mark. Using this whole survey technique of asking people what they want, do you normally need to give an incentive? Obviously people are busy, there are many things going on. Do you find that the effectiveness of the response, as well as the quantity of them, is tied to giving them an incentive to participate in your surveys?

Mark: It really depends. Depending on the relationship you have with the group of people that you are trying to survey, that's the basis of this. If you offer some kind of freebie, people will do the survey just to get the freebie, and therefore your statistics will be slanted from a bunch of people who should have never given you information. In other words, they just kind of answer and they don't care.

If you're not giving anything away, then you are getting people who really are interested in what you're doing and really want to give you correct information. So if you're really trying to base and judge something, don't give a freebie.

Participant: Not even something to do with a future product?

Mark: Well, you could do that. You could do something like that, but still that's towards the freebie thing. People are answering the question just to get something else, and it's not as pure.

Now, you're going to get smaller numbers. Instead of getting 50-75%, 80% response, you may only get 25% of the people, 20-25% to actually do the survey. However, you're going to get a better quality of the answers that you can base your business decisions on.

Another thing you might do, and I have done this frequently, is make it a surprise gift. In other words, you don't tell them what it is, so it creates a little curiosity.

You kind of have to test, test, test; those magic words that are so frustrating. But that's where you will see the big difference. I tend to, at this stage of the game, not give away something if I'm really trying to make a business decision, because I really only want people who are willing to do it just because I ask them for a favor.

I do a lot of people favors, freebies here and there and the other thing. Just every once in awhile I feel like it's fair game for me to ask for a favor back the other way.

Okay, that was an hour and a half. Did that go by quickly?

Why don't we take our first break, maybe about ten minutes Okay?

How Do You Reach The People Who Are Suffering From Information Overload When You Know That Your Product Is Superior To Similar Ones That They Have Already Purchased?

- Audio Two Transcript -

Mark: Okay, let's get back to it. That was Lou's first question. Let me pick another one that Lou had, because it looks like a pretty good one here, too.

I am just going to work my way through these questions and we are going to see where we land today and then tomorrow. Now, as we are talking, obviously, we are going down a lot of different paths, which is good. Is everybody comfortable with this? I'm having a good time, is everyone feeling like they're getting something out of this already? I hope so.

Yeah? Okay, great.

In the answers and the questions that we come up with, have another piece of paper where you write down the questions that pop in your head. They'll go away if you don't write them down, so write those down and we will get to those.

So we'll have ones from the pre-conference questions and then the questions that begat questions. We'll get to all of those, too.

So the next one is, "How do you reach the people who are suffering from information overload when you know that your product is superior to similar ones that they have already purchased?"

Information overload, has anybody ever suffered from that, that's got anything to do with Internet? Yeah.

[Laughter]

Back in '96 when I first started writing about Internet and Internet business and marketing stuff like that, I said, "You know, the Internet is the greatest wealth of knowledge ever assembled, and the biggest pile of trash ever collected in human history."

[Laughter]

That's the big problem we have, and the answer to that question is, you've got to be the sifter for your marketplace.

Does everyone understand what I just said? There is so much information out there and it all, on the surface level, seems like it's credible. But it's not. I mean some people just completely lie about whatever the topics are because they can. The reason being is they hide behind the computer screen and they think nobody knows where they are on the earth.

I've got news for you. I've ways I can track people down to where they live in India. I've had a situation where there was somebody who was getting in the way of my business, and I tracked him down to the door knocker. He was thinking he was hiding behind the computer screen and creating havoc with me. Well, I had news for him.

So when you are connected to the Internet you can be found. It just depends on how badly somebody wants to find you.

So the thing that I would recommend, and here's another thing, too. You need to consider this. If you're a business person, let's talk about brick and mortar business for a second. If you have a brick and mortar business in 1234 Main Street, Anytown, USA, are you going to give to the public your phone number?

Yes.

Are you going to give them your street address?

Yes.

Are you going to tell them what two city blocks you are on the corner of?

Yes.

If your business is on the Internet, does any of that really change?

It should not.

But back like in mid 90's and stuff, people were scared to death to give out their real name, their physical address, their phone number and how to contact them, which made no sense to me. Because as the business owner who is trying to attract business to you, you've got to take that risk.

Are there weirdos?

Yes!!

[Laughter]

Okay, there are weirdos in the brick and mortar world, too, and somehow you just have to deal with it.

Participant: I know everyone, when you say that, I assume that everyone somewhat registers with this whole identity theft concept and like you just said, crazy people all that and come online and grab you. Aren't their ways to kind of still protect yourself, if you are giving contact information out? For example, using a 1-800 number through some kind of service or third party, or Skype or VOIP?

Some kind of system where you are not necessarily putting it to your actual dwelling place. And/or if you could speak about using P.O. boxes, is that acceptable?

Mark: Well, I mean physical addresses are more credible than P.O boxes, even in direct mail. If you can use a physical address it just has more permanency than a P.O box.

Now what's to say that you can't go down to the corner at Mailboxes USA, and get yourself a box there, right? And you get to use the street address there. You just go down and your business address is their street address.

Yeah, you can have an 800 number or you can have a separate phone number that's tied to something that will just forward into your house or into your office, wherever it is. But that's a decision you have to make. I mean I know that it's a concern, but if you are going to do business you know you've got to deal with that.

You Must Help People With Their Information Overload

Information overload. So you have to be a sifter. You've got to be the one who goes out and puts on the hip boots, to go wading in this sea of overload and find all the good stuff and bring it back. That's how you deal with that. You've got to be the person who can make everything digestible, and what happens is you will get known for that and people will stop doing all their research so much and look forward to hearing from you.

Okay?

Now there's a reason why that works, and it's because you become the expert. You're the authority on the topic, so that when you speak people listen, right?

Any thoughts that come to mind after that?

By making good recommendations to other authorities, that's the other way to do it, too. In any given field you will have an opinion of who you think is good, and as you get to know your marketplace better and the other experts that are known in your marketplace, as you get to know them, you will get to know them, like them, trust them, like them, know them.

Or you may get to know them so well that you don't trust them anymore. That's what I mean. You went from know them, like them, trust them, to like them and then maybe just know them.

[Laughter]

Don't you know people in your life that way now? Yeah, you have friendships that were know you, like you, trust you, and now I don't trust him so much but I still kind of like him, but at a distance, right? You're not going to count on that relationship. Then there are some, where they've done something or things just have worked out to where you know who they are and you don't like to be around them anymore, and you surely don't trust them anymore.

Now I am just being honest here, okay? Because all relationships ebb and flow. But as you get to know your marketplace better and the players and as you take on the role of advocate, you have the power and position to refer people to other people. There will be some people that you are comfortable in referring them to, and then there are other people that you know it would be the worst thing possible for them to get into the clutches of that person. That's just because of how that person views the relationship with a customer.

Okay, now you don't have to go out of your way to say nasty things about other people, because nobody wants to hear that. They'll just think you're sour grapes, right? So the best thing you can say is nothing. Mom taught me that if I've got nothing nice to say, don't say anything at all.

So a lot of times that will say commentary much louder than if you actually said something. However, that's a difficult situation because as you get known as somebody that they know, like, and trust, they start trusting your opinion. They will ask you, "What about this person and that person?" It's kind of tough sometimes.

It's kind of more fun when they say, "In the field of this or this kind of specialty, who would you recommend?" It's an easier question to answer than, "What do you think about so-and-so?"

How To Find Prospective Customers For Your Products Or Services

"What's the best method or technique to find the prospective customers who have both the interest and the money to invest in what you are marketing, if you don't have a high search engine ranking and your pay per click option seems far too costly?"

Let's talk about how to find people. Let's go back even further; this is really, really basic. Write this down.

The big mistake people make is they create a product and try to sell it.

"What did you say, Mark?"

The big mistake is people create a product and try to sell it. It's much better to find people who want something-write it down-who were already buying it from someplace and who would like to buy more of it repeatedly.

Then the easy way is to go find somebody who has already created that product and service-that's the second step, with one qualification-and knows how to sell it.

So that's the second area. And the third step is put the two together: the buyer and seller

So when somebody asks me, "What's the quickest way I know of to make money in the Internet?" What's the quickest way I know of making money period? It's to find somebody who wants to buy something, find somebody who wants to sell something and knows how to sell it, and put the two together.

Can it really be that simple? The answer is what?

Yes!

Now, is there infrastructure that has to be built to be able to do that?

Yes, but Internet infrastructure sure beats them having to build factories and office buildings, and having to have the capital to do that kind of thing.

Now where can we find these people? Well let's talk about fishing for a second. Where do fish live? I know it sounds pretty simple but I am trying to make a big point here.

Where do fish live? In the water. Do you go looking for fish on dry land? No. If you want to find fish, you are going to have to look in the water. All the ones that I have ever seen are in water.

Okay that's number one. We're going to have to find a pond, right? Now the next thing is we have to figure out what? If you're going to catch a fish, bait. What do they like to eat? How many of you know the book, and write that book down in case if you haven't read it. Or if you have read it, I guarantee you ought to read it again like ten times. How to Win Friends and Influence People" by Dale Carnegie. How many of you have read it?

How many of you have read it twice? Three? Five? Okay. You need to get it to where I see at least five times.

In that book Mr. Carnegie talks about catching fish and it's a great story. He says, "Me, I prefer strawberries and cream, but I know the fish like big, juicy, fat, wiggly worms. Now if I want to catch fish, I am going to give them juicy, fat, wiggly worms. Then when I get home and relax, I am going to have myself strawberries and cream.

Now there in that simple story lies marketing wisdom that's priceless. That fish, your marketplace, will bite on the bait that they like, not on what you like.

Your marketplace does not care about you and what you like; that's a harsh reality. But you've got to flip yourself around to be on the same side of the table. Am I repeating myself for a good reason here? The same side of the table so you can be the advocate to your marketplace; so you can understand their hopes, dreams wishes, goals, fears, doubts, nightmares, disasters.

So you can have the empathy, right? Which is different from sympathy. Empathy-"I know how you feel, I am like you." So you can communicate as one with them, as a true friend.

So we've got step two as the bait. We have a pond and there are fish in it, and we have bait that the fish likes. What's the third thing that has to happen before we catch a fish?

Yeah, you have to put the bait in the water. Can you make the fish eat the bait? No. The fish has to be hungry.

Now isn't that what you would like? You would like to have a pond full of prospects or customers; just a barrel full, right? And you'd like to have the bait that they love to eat; and would you like to have them hungry? So that as soon as you pop that bait in there, they will jump on it? Now that's fishing!

Did you know that there's a difference between fishing and catching. Who likes to go fishing? Who likes to go catching?! Yeah, that's for me! Right? Barrel of fish, bait that they like, and they haven't seen food in a week. Now that's catching!

Who said business needs to be a challenge, right? You can go get your challenges someplace else. Business needs to be systems that you set up that work and work and work and work based on finding the market; what do they want? Give it to them when they're hungry and then they'll buy it from you.

Now have you noticed that I haven't talked anything about Web design and I haven't talked anything about autoresponders, I haven't talked anything about Internet infrastructure, I haven't talked anything about building an e-book, doing recordings, all the technological parts of Internet business. There's a real good reason for that, and we can get into some of that, but the real big reason is none of that stuff matters unless you get all this other stuff right.

You can spend a gob of money building Web sites, getting all the server stuff together, getting all the infrastructure together, buying traffic and all this kind of stuff. But when somebody shows up, if they're not the right fish and you don't have the right bait and if they're not hungry, guess what's going to happen? Zippo.

And I don't care what approach to Internet marketing you take, it doesn't matter. Unless somebody is wanting to take an action before they show up at your doorstep; in other words, they're hungry for something, they want something. Unless you've got an idea of what they want, so that you can show it to them, and then you make an actionable situation where you help them take that step, if that's not in place then all the bells and whistles do not matter.

Now the bells and whistles and all that stuff can enhance our simple little scenario. Just like when I was little guy I used to go cane pole fishing. Talk about a simple setup, right? I mean you have a hook, a bobber, a worm and a 10-foot cane pole with a string on the end of it. But do you know what? You catch fish that way. Or you can have a big rig and a big 36' boat and go out in the ocean, and you can catch fish that way. That's just bigger toys, right? Bells and whistles. But the game, the psychology, is the same thing. The want, the bait, and the action, and that's the process. Does that make sense? Okay.

Because if you think in these simple terms, you will do okay. You will finally get it and things will start happening for you. If you get hung up on the technology you will just spin your wheels, and you'll wonder why this stuff doesn't work. Has anybody ever had a Web site that just didn't do anything? Now you know why.

If you will go back and analyze the things that have not worked for you in these simple terms, I think you will spot it immediately. Maybe you bought some automatic pilot Web site from somebody else, right? You had no clue what the marketplace was, you just bought it, you got to put it up on your domain, and somehow people are supposed to find it and buy from it.

You have no rapport with the marketplace. They don't know you, they don't like you, they don't trust you. You are no different from anybody else who has a site just like this, right?

Why should somebody buy from you rather than somebody else? You've got to answer that question, by the way. You need to write that down. That's called unique selling proposition, unique selling advantage, or whatever we want to call. It's how you are going to position yourself as unique in the marketplace.

Lou, you come up with good questions, once I get rolling, huh?

Now let's talk about that stuff for a second; unique selling proposition, unique selling advantage. It's positioning yourself uniquely in the marketplace so that people can see you as the obvious choice to do business with. Remember that book that Elsom wrote, The Obvious Expert?

By the way, if you haven't got that you can get the e-book version if you go to www.Obvious-Expert.com/ebook That's one of those PDF digital downloads. You can also buy it off of www.Amazon.com if you want a hard copy. The price is the same. You go to Amazon.com and just search for "Obvious Expert" and it will pop up.

Participant: I guess my question is for those copies of his book that are being sold through Amazon. Those are being done through a fulfillment house; it would be helpful to have the information on the fulfillment house.

Mark: Okay, yeah, I can give you a little bit of stuff on that. Actually, Elsom has batches of like 1,000 of them printed up. He actually gives them to Amazon, or something. I don't know how he sets up that. But there's another one that's more interesting. He's really up on this stuff. He's my source on this kind of publishing.

Go to Lightning, you know, like crash, boom, thunder, www.LightningSource.com and you can have printed up and distributed and delivered, onesies-twosies off of this site. Full blown published books and that kind of stuff.

And here's what's cool about it--and tie into the big book sellers. Get the number, the ISBN or number or whatever it is. Get all that done and I think there is setup fee maybe, I can't remember. Maybe it's $100 or something like that. The cost for this kind of thing, to be able to, when somebody orders it or you call up and say, "I need this done and ship it out to this person." I mean, it's very nominal, what it costs.

Anyway, check that out. I think you will find it fascinating what can be done these days.

So you get your whole book out in a format where they can print it. They've got all the guides and details. You have cover art and the whole process, and you give them all that information. They keep it in place and then when the order comes through or you send in the order, they print that thing up and put it out the door. So it's print-on-demand, is what it's all about.

They have various things. Just go there and you will see all kinds of stuff. Yes, I mean it's like at the bookstore, like a paperback you just pull off the shelf. It looks like that kind of thing. I don't know if they do hardback or not; apparently not. It's like a Barnes & Noble or Waldenbooks kind of thing.

Three steps, we have talked about that . Where did we leave off? You've got me off there. USP-Unique Selling Proposition. Okay, so you've got to be unique.

How To Enter Your Market Niche On The Should Of Your Competitors

Now let's go back to some of your questions, Lou.

One of the things that I like to do when I am entertaining moving into a marketplace, is I make what I call a competitive grid. I will find the top three, four, or five competitors. Typically five. I look through what they're offering the marketplace; I go to all their sales pages and if I can, I get their products. I will do like a benefit chart. I go through all their stuff and just list, "Okay, this one offers this benefit, this benefit, this benefit," and on and on and on. then I will look at the next one and maybe they offer some benefits that the first one didn't do, so I will have another column for that benefit.

So do you see where I am going with this? I make this big grid of all the benefits being offered by the five top competitors. Now what you'll see, and you check off next to their name, do they include this benefit in their offer? You'll see that some have more checks than others and some have more holes in their offers, compared to the other ones.

Now I make another column that's going to be me. So the last column or the first column, whichever way you want to do it-the benefit's kind of go left to right, like a list all the way down. Then the five have a column and there are checks whether they or not they have included that benefit. The last column is going to be my product, and guess what? I have all the boxes checked, even though I don't have the product yet. Okay?

Now how is that for a starting point? I have researched all the competitors, I know what their strengths are, I know where the holes are in each one, and then I am going to make mine contain all the benefits where there are no holes. That's going to be the starting point. That's the minimum performance I am shooting for.

Now if I work on this project, don't you think that I can include all those things that I see out in the marketplace? The answer is yes. Don't you think I have enough creativity that I can kind of mix things together and come up with something even better, and even add a few bells and whistles to the whole thing?

So that when I jump into the marketplace, I've got something really different and unique. It's all of theirs and more. I mean, you literally can say that. Okay? So that's the way to enter a marketplace. That way you are not having to come in and say, "Me too! Me, too!"

Even if you did nothing more than consolidate all the benefits of the other places, you would be one up on them on the "Me, too!" stuff, because instead of buying five different packages you can buy just this one and have it all.

But wait, there is more! Because we didn't stop there. We did this and this and this and this and this and this and packaged it into the thing.

So that's product design in a nutshell. I mean that's a three-day workshop in itself, just talking about all the different things you can do with products.

What Kind Of Products Can We Easily Make That We Can Sell On The Internet?

Why don't we take a moment to do that? What kind of products can we make that people will buy from us?

Do you want to talk about physical products or information products?

Information products.

Okay, what makes the Internet work?

Information.

Can you buy hard products off the Internet?

Yes. If you're selling hard products on the Internet you are going to have to deal with UPS, FedEx and US Postal, okay? You will get to know those people really well.

Now you may have a fulfillment house and you will get to know those people very well, too. Then they will take care of, "What can Brown do for you?"

But in the information product world we can either go digital, with audios and PDF books and that kind of stuff, or we can press them into CDs and DVDs and print books and all this kind of stuff. Yeah, you're going to have fulfillment there. Chances are if you go fulfillment there, you will have somebody who manufactures that for you and stocks them, so when you have orders to ship out, you can just send it to them and they will take care of that for you. Okay? So that's still very hands-off and Internet-oriented.

What kind of products can we do? Let's just start a list.

How-to information.

What format can we do this in? PDF e-books. Okay, what else?

Audio. MP3s are easy, CDs are good.

Video. Either on DVD or Camtasia, which is screen capture off the computer.

What other formats? E-course by e-mail.

What else can we do? Teleseminars, teleconferences. They can be live, they can be recorded and repackaged as audios.

Software development. Yeah, let's talk about software development.

How about Web conferencing, where you get audio and video? So now we are able to do video recording by way of screen capture, and package that up. Of course, that's got video and audio; you could actually make two products out of that, right?

It's one of the things I did last weekend at the List Building Conference. I did Camtasia, I just had the Camtasia thing running on anything that went on on-screen. It recorded the video of it and it also recorded the audio track. So what I'm doing when I get back, I have to edit just a little bit, with the start and stops and things like that. What I am going to do is to edit the video; and of course the audio gets edited at the same time. Then I am going to save the audio as a separate thing.

So I will have video which includes the audio, where people can watch it, and then I will also have just the audio track that people can play on their MP3 players while they go walking or driving or whatever else it is they do. So I gave them a couple of different formats.

Okay, what else could I do with audios? I could have them transcribed. So we can have those transcribed and then it will be in the written format. So out of one event, one moment in time, we could have three products.

Now you can sell them separately or you can sell them as a bundle, right? Because some people like to sit in front of their computer and watch video, other people prefer to hear it-repetition while they're walking or driving in a car, or whatever it is. And other people prefer to pull away from technology and just sit down and read paper, or they could sit at the computer and read the words, too. Right?

So there's four. We give them printed-on-paper version, we give them the PDF version, we give them the audio version, and we give them the video version, all from one moment in time.

What other kinds of products could we develop?

Podcasting; with all those MP3s you could put them up and do a podcast thing. It's a great way to get traffic in video too, you can do that.

Blogging. You can make a blog out of this information.

A membership site where you put the contents in there. What kind of content do we want? Actionable content. Do not settle for content or relevant content. You've got to go for actionable content. Lead people to the next step.

Lead people to the next step.

What other kind of product can we make out of information? What's that?

Articles. Okay, articles are great for literally getting your name out there. It's not advertising as in the old days of getting your name out there. But articles help establish you as an expert, and also it's the thing that search engines tend to like, because somebody who can write is an expert and search engines believe that if you are an expert then you are worthy of traffic coming your way from them.

A Simple Explanation Of How Search Engines Work

Do you want to know how a search engine works? Are you are ready? Everybody point to the ceiling. Everybody point to the floor. Everybody point to the wall. Look around; don't move. Look at where everybody is pointing.

Isn't that interesting? We all knew what the real ceiling was, we all knew what the real floor was, but when I asked you to point to the wall, everybody points in different directions. Therein lies what a search engine does. It relies on users to tell the search engine where the wall is.

There is a guy who teaches these concepts, Harold Anderson; he is an ISS member. He's been with us from the beginning and Harold is a crackerjack at these search engine games. That's the basis; I mean, talk about me getting basic, but as soon as Harold showed me that, it all made sense. You know all these linking strategies that everybody talks about that are so complicated? And it can get complicated, but the simplicity is, would you like to be the person known as "ceiling"? Where everybody knows that when somebody says, "Where do I go for ceiling?" everybody points there! Okay?

All over the Internet, everybody has a link on their site and the word that says, "ceiling," and underneath that link, underneath those words is a hyperlink. Everybody knows what they look like, right? And underneath that it's got your Web site address, and when they click it they go to you as the ceiling place.

The problem is when you start asking people, "Where is the best wall?" And people start pointing in all different directions. That's where your strategy comes in, how do you get more people pointing to your wall? The person who has got the most other

93

people pointing to you, wins.

I'm stealing Harold's thunder here. If you ever hear him talk, you'll hear him talk about this, I'm sure. He talks about in the last presidential election; Kerry and Bush, right? To me it's not Republicans and Democrats, it's Republocrats, okay? They're all the same. But if you searched for the word "waffle," where would you end up?

The number one spot was Kerry's Web site, because he was known as what? He is always waffling, right? And what was the one for Bush? Miserable failure. And these words did not appear on the Web sites.

So if you spend all your time trying to optimize your pages, that's not where the action is. The action is what everybody else says about you. Just like in dealing with people, it doesn't matter what I say about me, right? It matters what everybody else says about me.

What's more powerful? What you say about yourself or what other people say about you to somebody else? It's the second. It's more powerful what other people say about you.

The same thing in linking with search engines. You can spend all the time and energy on your Web site trying to optimize it, doing all the tricks and everything. The problem is, I am guessing 80% of it is going to be what other people think of your Web site and whether or not they will point links back to you on certain keyword phrases that you would be like to be known for. That's it.

How did I go down that road?

Articles. Okay, so articles are good because you can pull out keywords. And the search engines like articles because they like experts and if you get known for certain keywords, they will point back to you.

Information products, podcasting, blogging, teleseminars we talked about, right?

How about events? How about weekend events, one-day events or three-day events, or week events. Or Alan's doing something cool; Bechtel. He's doing these things like every Saturday; like 8 Saturdays in a row or something like that. It's his Webinar series.

I was the part of first one and pretty soon I will be starting up here. That's where you can hear people talk that normally you would have to travel to a conference to see, but Alan's using that Webinar technology, that Web conference technology. That's where I had a camera on top of my computer screen and I just sat and gave a presentation. Then my mug is on everybody's screen and people got to hear me talk about whatever the topic was; "Ten Things That You Have to Have in Place to Do Business on the Internet," I think was mine. It was just a couple of months ago.

So he lines up guest speakers that normally you would see only at a conference, but now you sit in your skivvies in front of your computer screen, and you plug in and you listen and learn. This is not a new concept. He's just aggressively done it. He likes the idea.

Now what's the downside of that? You don't really meet the people, right? And you don't get to meet the people who are sitting next to you. You don't get to go to breakfast, lunch, and dinner with the people for a couple of days. Okay?

The good news is you get to hear the words and you get to see somebody's picture, but the bad news is that it really doesn't develop the relationship. Okay?

Now it's kind of a good first step for a lot of people, so maybe that's what it can develop into. Maybe it's actionable content that's being developed. And maybe the next step is people that would actually be that interested and have a good experience from that;

maybe they would want to come to a live event.

Should You Be Going To Live Events?

How many of you go to live events? Now I realize this one's a cheap date.

[Laughter]

I mean, this is a really good deal and I am having fun, believe me. This is an experiment for me because I am thinking about doing this around the country. As long as they are fun and as long as these nice people like you show up, it will be fun to do. But live events, if you haven't been to one before-how many have not been to a live event other than what you are at right here today?

This is your first one? Great. Everybody make sure you get to know him, okay? That way he will really get the value out of this weekend, because everybody else understands the value of going to a live event. It's where you get to meet the people and start the relationships.

On those Web conferencing things, it's terrific information but you just don't get to meet the people. It's nice to get away from wherever you work; the workplace. Whether it be home or office or wherever it is, get away from that so that you can focus specifically on something for a few days in the conferences.

So live events are great. You could put together a coaching program. See, all these things build on one another, one another, one another. So when somebody comes to you initially for that freebie, and a humble freebie starts it all, doesn't it? It starts that relationship.

Now let's move it into another area. How many of you ever had a romantic relationship? Good.

How did that relationship start? I mean, can you really think back at the instant that it happened? I do this frequently.

I mean the very first thing that happened. Yeah, wasn't there a glance? Can you remember that far back into it? There was a glance where two sets of eyes for a time, I mean just a millisecond, were in contact, and all of a sudden there were no other eyes in the whole world, were there?

In that moment in time, if you can freeze it, everything else left and that was the beginning of that relationship. Then look what happened. What was the next step? It was something very, very, small wasn't it? Maybe a smile, and it progresses in little, bitty, baby steps. Now what happens if you ask that other person to take a step bigger than they're willing to go?

Screech.... the brakes go on fast, right?

[Laughter]

Then what do you have to do if you want to continue that relationship? You've got to backup, and maybe backup a little bit further than where you were, and get another start going again. Then instead of that leap you were asking, what we have to do in that leap? More little baby steps. That's the way it is in any relationship.

We talked about joint ventures a little while ago, and I am telling you, if you are running into resistance it's because you are asking the other party to take too big a step. They're not ready for that yet. So you are going to have to back up.

Of course, we're ready for it, right? Because we want it.

Guess what? That's called being selfish. As a marketer you have to get rid of that. As a marketer, whose side of the table do you have to be sitting at all the time?

This is like out-of-body experience, folks. I know you want things to go your way, but to get them to go your way, what do you have to do? You actually have to care about the customers and prospects more than you do yourself. If you will get your mind on that side of the table, things will start going your way. It's when all you do is think about you and what you want out of it, that's when you are going to run into biggest frustration.

Does that make sense?

Guess what? That's hard to do, because why? Because we are humans and we've got emotions, too. But as a marketer, you've got to be able to flip that off, go sit on the side of your marketplace, and have empathy on their side. Help them find what they want. You'll get what you want; you just have to delay the gratification.

Any other questions?

Participant: I've been in your 12 Days of Christmas and I opted in with a couple of other adventurers. The e-mail overload is incredible because everybody wants you on their e-mail list. I don't know, I mean, I wind up ignoring virtually everyone unless they have a really good subject line.

Beyond that, you were talking about advertising your business. I must have gotten into some "yes" with my Yahoo address, because the spam is incredible. The bad part about it is, they do put the spam in the spam folder, which is really good, but then some of my good stuff winds up there, too. So I wind up going though all those damn spams, like 500 messages a day, and I don't have time for all this.

So my only conclusion is that I protect my Comcast address like gold and I change my Yahoo address, which means that I have to e-mail everybody on Yahoo that has my address and get them to change my address.

That's still more time. So is there any way to avoid that kind of stuff? Especially once you've gotten a Web site up and you want everybody to have your addresses, I mean all your prospects.

Are you following what I mean? I am just tired going through this stuff.

Mark: Sure. The situation of signing up for all those freebies, that's the tradeoff obviously. Right? And more people have figured out, "Yeah, I'll open up a junk address and have all the stuff sent over there and get all the goodies, and get back to that address to see what other kind of stuff is being sent. Then if I like that person, then I'll re-subscribe. Maybe not through my main address but at least to a more treasured freebie address." Right?

You have to do that to protect yourself.

The Infrastructure Of Internet Marketing

Now let's talk about Internet stuff for a second. We're going to talk about the infrastructure. One of the big problems with Yahoo, and I have just been through this over the last couple of months; it's getting harder and harder, if you've heard, to get your e-mail delivered.

One of the situations over at Yahoo is that there is a site called DeliveryMonitor.com. Maybe we can take a visit over there; maybe this afternoon. Remind me and I will take you over there and you can look in my account. DeliveryMonitor.com. What they did is they set up dummy accounts, like ten dummy accounts at each of the top 12 ISPs like Yahoo and AOL, Bellsouth, MSM, Hotmail, and all these kinds of things. You get to see your deliverability to these places.

Now the situation at Yahoo is e-mail goes into Yahoo; let's say somebody signs up to get stuff from me and I send them e-mail. Instead of just following the directions at the bottom of every e-mail that I send out, it says there, "If you don't want any more of this, just click here and you're gone."

But, no. They go, "Oh this is spam." After they're done reading they stick it over and they click spam. Now what they don't know is that anybody who does want to get e-mail from me, if there's enough of those, automatically my mail goes to the spam box and that's what is happening to you. Stuff that you want to get is being filtered over to that spam box, even though you never did anything. Right?

Participant: I noticed that only certain people. There's a Juan Carlos that's pretty good and I've been getting his stuff. And Platinum Sellers from eBay, they wind up in the spam thing occasionally.

Mark: Yeah. And see, there's nothing that you did. It's because other Yahoo users have said, "This is spam," and put them into their spam box. Yahoo assumes that it ought to be going there,

Participant: Yeah, they're not careful like I am.

[Laughter]

Mark: That's right. Now the way to fix that is that you need to go into your e-mail thing in Yahoo and whitelist them. And it will get delivered.

Now as a publisher, one of your concerns is, "How do I get my deliverability up?" What you have to do, and it's getting harder and harder, number one, you really do have to have your own server. I mean you don't have to own it but at least you are the only thing happening on that server.

Most people started out with a shared server situation, and on your Web host account you probably share that computer server. Does everybody know what a server is? It's a computer that's attached to the Internet that dishes out your Web pages to everybody.

You probably share that with 100-200 other businesses, and if one of them does something stupid, you get blamed for it, too. That's because it's coming out of that same computer. So the next step up is to have a virtual server, where maybe you share it with 10-20 people. It's sectioned off, like partitioned like on a hard drive kind of thing, where it'll have an IP address and you have a little bit more of it to yourself. You're isolated from boneheads; that's what it is.

[Laughter]

People who do stupid stuff like spam and create these kinds of problems.

That will last you for awhile until you get your business going and you are driving a lot of traffic, or maybe sending some portion of e-mail and it's going to affect that server enough that the people who share that virtual server with you will start complaining. That's because their sites will start slowing down because of the volume of business that you do.

Then your next step is to have your own server and you want to make sure that your domain name that you mail from matches the server name, because that's what Yahoo is looking for. It's not wrong that your server has a different name, domain name, and the main domain name you would have on there. It's just that Yahoo wants to see them match up.

I had to go through this here about a month ago, just to iron all this stuff out.

Then Yahoo will put you through about a two-week period where they will check every e-mail coming through to Yahoo users. And they will spot check and see what kind of business you do. If they think that you are clean then they will so called "whitelist" you so that you won't automatically go to the spam box.

So now after going through all that process of changing my main server and two-week thing with Yahoo, I get 100% deliverability to the Yahoo boxes; unless somebody has specifically stuck me in their spam box, personally has put me there.

Participant: I got smarter on the last 12 Days and I set up a separate Comcast account. Everything just goes in there and I can ignore it for awhile if I have the time, rather than coming into my main e-mail. So as I have done your JV's and other ones, I'm an efficiency engineer and I just skinny it down. So it takes me less time to do all that stuff. I mean it gets overwhelming to be on that mailing list.

Mark: That's the first thing you do when you sign up for that stuff. I do the same thing. I have some accounts that that's where it goes first, and I go in there and read some stuff. If somebody is making some sense and I want to know more, I will go over to a different one and eventually they make it up to my personal account.

Participant: Yeah, that's what we want to know. What do you do with those kinds of things?

Mark: That's exactly the same thing.

Participant: Okay.

Mark: I mean, you've got to protect yourself against stuff that you don't want.

Participant: I just wanted to add something that's sort of related, just in case you have an answer to this. I'm sure everybody would love to hear it. I have quite a few Web sites and one of them I consider has a very prime name. Unfortunately I am now in a situation where I am going to probably have to take the whole site down because spammers has started sending all kinds of trash using my domain name, as so-and-so from my domain name.

I have already stripped off all of my regular e-mail addresses from that site. I've put up a big notice on my home page saying, "If you're receiving spam mail, it's not coming from me." But the hosting service tells me they can't do anything about it. I was wondering if you had ever come across anything like that before and if you have any solutions.

Mark: Yeah, I have; it happened to me a couple or 3 or 4 months ago. There was a security flaw on my server. There was a script that I got from somebody and whoever wrote it put something in it so they can get in there and mail from my server and have everything emanate from my domain. And I mean, they sent out awful stuff. They didn't send it out to my list; they just sent it to whoever, the millions they go out and harvest e-mail addresses.

So yeah, there is stuff that your hosting company can do. It was two or three weeks of running all kinds of security checks and going back and forth with a particular company who was receiving a lot of it and banning the e-mail. They had some insight into it, and we went back and forth where my guy said there was nothing on it and these guys said, "You need to check this, this, and this." Eventually it got worked out, because I'm going, "Come on, guys!"

Participant: Yeah, well that particular hosting company that I have that site on tells me that there is nothing that they can do about it. That's why I've reached the point where I'm going to have to take it down.

Mark: No, but that may be a true statement. There's nothing that they can do about it. You might want to move it to a different hosting company. The thing is that your domain name is tied to a server computer and that server computer has the IP address and if you change that, you can change the IP address of that domain name. You don't want to do that too much or people see you as being a problem kind of person. But if you are having this kind of problem, that's what you need to be doing; keeping the domain name, changing the IP address, and moving to a different server.

Participant: All right. So as long as I move that to one of my other hosting servers, a different company, then this should stop.

Mark: It may work. Now there may be something, some script on your domain that's on there, that's causing this security hole.

Participant: If it's there, it was put there by someone, some spammer, and I will evaluate that before I reload.

Mark: Yeah, but the problem is if you transfer all the information from one server to another, guess what's going to go with it?

Participant: Yeah, that's what I said. I will make sure I clean all the pages before putting them back up.

Mark: Right. You may have to just upload everything all over again and watch out for that kind of stuff. If it comes back again there's something on there that they're getting into.

Folks, if you are hosting with ElCheapoHosting.com, you're asking for it. Or it may be your most expensive one that you are overpaying, too.

[Laughter]

Do you want a recommendation for hosting?

Participants: Yeah.

Mark: Okay. Do you want an affiliate link?

[Laughter]

www.Hunteridge.com/hosting.htm You can go either way I don't care. Steve is a great guy. He has a lot different hosting packages from $10 a month up to your own dedicated server and all points in between, and he can speak your language. He knows all the technical stuff, but this is; I've been through like five different hosting companies over the years and I have been with Steve two years, I think now. And I have loved it, and I could not say that about any of the other ones.

It was always fighting. I could never understand it. I'm the customer, I am paying money, and why doesn't somebody care? Anytime I had a problem it was always something that I had done wrong until I proved to them that it was always something they had screwed up. Invariably that was the case. That's the first thing they want to say, is that it's something you did, some script that you put on there.

Now in many cases that can be right, but in my case that wasn't the case. Now I have Steve, who when I have a problem; I am on the dedicated server and he manages it for me. So if there's any problem for me, he's the detective on the thing. So it really saves a lot.

Participant: Since you are on this topic, when you have switched in the past your hosting, I imagine you had multiple domains at that host?

Mark: Yeah.

Participant: Did you have a lot of trouble switching it over all at one time? Was that a two-day delay, that whole pagination situation?

Mark: No.

Participant: Because I have about eight different accounts that people are paying me to host, and I want to switch over. It's just like you're saying; I have a cheap, junkie one and I need to get out of that.

Mark: No, it's getting a lot quicker because, what's that clearing house? ICan or whatever it's called? It's a lot quicker of propagating the domains with the IP addresses and the DNS stuff. I mean like at GoDaddy, you can set up a domain and I mean 15 minutes later it's finding your Web site. It used to take 24-48 hours to do that. So it's similar when you flip from hosting companies; it's getting a lot quicker. But yeah, sometimes you could be down for a day.

Now you could also not do it all at once. Set up your account and then you could flip a couple of domains one day, so that you are not completely out of business if you have income streams. Do you see what I mean?

Participant: Yeah.

Mark: By the way, when you do this always want to open up your new hosting account and get everything set there, get a great relationship with those people, because this is the best it's going to be. When they first get your money and you haven't asked for anything.

[Laughter]

So everybody is happy. The marriage has begun. The next thing that's going to happen is you're going to be transferring your domains and all your HTML files, all your scripts, and all your databases and that kind of stuff, over there. I would not try to have them transfer everything at once.

Now you're still going to have it on your old host. You're not going to give that one up. You've got to keep that for about a month. You still want to store it there in case you've got problems over at the new place. And you want to make sure that this is a smooth transition, so your main Web site, maybe that's not the first one you want to transfer, right? You want to transfer some of your lesser ones over first to make sure that transfer goes smoothly. Does that make sense? Nice and conservative. Then you see how things are going and how these tech guys are doing and working for you, and how quick things are happening. That will give you an idea of when to flip over your bigger sites. Especially like the ones you e-mail out of, because that's where you're going to typically have the bigger problems.

If you have an e-mail script on your site, those are most likely some of the most complicated scripts because you've got cron jobs running and MYSQL databases and the script is more involved, and stuff like that. So when that thing flips over, that's usually where you have some what I call plumbing problems. It it's going to happen it happens on that kind of stuff. Does that help out?

Okay.

Participant: I would like to ask you about shopping carts verses PayPal and ClickBank and AWeber.

Mark: Okay. Payment processors first. The easy way to go, if you want to have your own affiliate program, the easiest way to go is ClickBank. Because you become a vendor for about $40; $49.95 or something like that. It's a one time fee. They take out 7 ½% plus $1 on every transaction.

Now you also access a lot of affiliates very quickly that way. Now, don't count on affiliates finding you. You still have to go looking for affiliates.

PayPal is another way to take payments, obviously, and that's real easy and quick to setup. It usually takes a couple of days because you have to tie it to like a bank account, and stuff like that.

The affiliate software that I would suggest if you are going to use PayPal, is something called IdevAffiliate. You get it at IDevDirect.. It's a $99 one time fee. It will handle like affiliate banners and e-mailing them and keeping in touch and you can have unlimited products and it's soup-to-nuts. It ties into PayPal very easily and it ties into lot of different payment processes very easily, too.

So IDevDirect.com is one, and you can go to www.Hunteridge.com/idev.htm Yeah, that will get you there.

And pick that up. I use that for one of my affiliate programs. I had it customized to where it does ClickBank, also. That's a whole different story, but IDevDirect is terrific. It will put you into, he has a bunch of different payment processors that you can tie it to. PayPal is one that's easy, so that you can have that up and running just in a couple of days.

That installs on your server and it's a one-time payment; you don't have to pay them monthly. It manages your affiliate program.

Now the next thing you're going to need is an autoresponder system. If you're starting out, I would recommend AWeber. And that's at AWeber, or at www.Hunteridge.com/aweber.htm

[Laughter]

Participant: Hi. My name is Ryan. A friend of mine, Mike Nicholas, referred me to a program called www.BypassPublisher.com He said that's a very good program.

Mark: Yeah, that would be a terrific one. That's one of the ones I developed.

[Laughter]

We'll talk about, the only downside right now is it's off the market. I'm having it rewritten, the script. Let me tell you about BypassPublisher. That's what it's called. It combines the traditional e-mail autoresponder system, where you can do sequential e-mails and broadcast e-mails, in other words like published once a week. Or set them up in a series and have unlimited lists, unlimited subscribers, based on obviously your storage on your server. It will work 24/7 for you.

Now, it does traditional e-mail, just like we all know and love for the last few years. Now the reason it's called Bypass because the biggest problem that you have is that between you and your reader, your customer, your subscriber, your prospect, you've got something called an ISP. Such as Yahoo, AOL, Bellsouth, Comcast; and they have taken the position that they're going to protect their customers from spammers. And because of that, you, the good guy, get caught in that, too. You can't get your e-mail delivered, either.

So what Bypass does is it bypasses it. It goes directly from my computer server, my Web site, directly to your computer where the message is not blocked at all. It lets the people know, "You have a message on Mark's server, specifically for you," whether it be broadcast or sequential follow-ups.

Now you would think that I am controlling what shows up on your computer. I'm not, because if at any time you don't want to hear from me you click a button and I'm gone. I have no say-so. It's not like we have to have an unsubscribe link. That's not the situation. You subscribe and unsubscribe by clicking a button.

So it's based on RSS technology, but a super-duper kind of RSS technology where it's personalized. In other words, I can include your name and contact information, or whatever information I get from you. I can personalize messages to you, both in a broadcast and sequential follow-ups, so that it works just like the e-mail autoresponders that we know and use now.

It actually does both in tandem. So you can send out both a traditional e-mail and you can send out the Bypass RSS. See, the value of sending out the RSS side is that all your pages can look like Web pages without having to go through filters at the ISPs. Those will assume that if you're sending HTML messages, that you are doing commerce and if you are doing commerce you've got to be a spammer. Right? I mean, who would possibly want HTML? I'm being facetious here.

Participant: It will do us both a favor if you would put all your affiliate links in an e-mail to the attendees. If we're going to need these services anyway, we might as well do it through you.

Mark: [Laughter]

Well, that'd be sweet of y'all. Thank you. Thank you.

BypassPublisher.com is one way to get to it. We are working on it; I am having it upgraded and getting a couple of new bells and whistles put into it. We are doing a whole new version update. It's not just an upgrade, but a whole version update.

Now a thing to talk about, the e-mail side of it works fine. It's just couple of bells and whistles I want to add to it, from customers. Other people are already using it, so I get feedback from them and we build it into the newer version. It was really ahead of its time, because I had this available for two and a half years, two years, maybe. I can't remember.

How many of you use an RSS reader? Right, less than five percent, and that's the way it is in the world. Now how many of you have heard of the letters RSS? Okay, a lot of people have heard of RSS, it means Really Simple Syndication. That's what the world is saying. There are a couple of other definitions, but Really Simple Syndication. Meaning that I can create content and put it up on my site in a format that if you subscribe to this content, you can actually plug it into your site and have it show up on your pages.

That way you don't have to create the content. You can get it from me. Thus syndication, just like AP Press and UPI does that with the print newspapers, right? It's the same concept, except now we're using the technology to where I print something or I publish something and it shows up on your Web site automatically.

How many of you have blogs? Most people are starting to do blogs. The reason search engines love blogs, and people are loving blogs, is because guess what? It's built on RSS technology. Blogs are RSS. That's why you are able to pull information out of blogs and have it show up at different places, and that kind of stuff.

So the BypassPublisher, one of the reasons it was kind of ahead of its time was because so few people were using RSS readers. But Internet Explorer 7 has RSS reader built into it. So it will be seamless once people start getting Internet Explorer 7. That means that 80% of the world now has RSS readers, of which it makes BypassPublisher, the timing is perfect for this.

So you'll be able to have subscribers in various lists and niche lists, and all that kind of stuff, and you'll be able to communicate directly to them, 100% deliverability. None of this stinky ISP filtering stuff. None of this whitelisting stuff. If somebody subscribes, they're a subscriber. If they want to unsubscribe they click a button on their computer and no longer do you get delivered to their RSS reader. So that's going to be exciting.

Now there are some other people who have kind of caught onto the idea and they've developed a few things along the same lines. But watch for that.

So that should be hopefully later this summer that we have that ready to go.

So AWeber, if you're going to do traditional, AWeber has got an RSS side to it. I mean, I don't know if it is personalized, I am not sure how it works. But AWeber is good. They like you to do what's called a double opt-in, to make sure that somebody who says that they want to subscribe, to ask them again, which I can't stand double opt-in.

I went on and on about it last weekend, down at our conference on List Building. The reason is, one of the guys, over the weekend people actually created content and built subscription pages, and built like freebies to give away. It was a really good weekend. Anyway, this one guy did one and we did a test on it, and I signed up on the screen here and I didn't get the e-mail. The confirmation e-mail. Now here's somebody who was at your site, filled in the form; I didn't get the e-mail nor did I get the freebie that was promised to me. How's our relationship so far? Not good!

So I finally went in there and filled it out again, and it finally came to me. I had to click the thing, it took me back to a page, now I'm double opted in and now it says, "Check your e-mail for the message." I have to go back and check my e-mail again and there's the message. Then to get whatever it was, I had to click this and go back to his Web site again. So how many times have I had to do this? I've been back and forth to his Web site three times just to get something for free. If I wasn't really interested, how long am I willing to play this game?

Participant: Yeah. With AWeber is not mandatory that you double opt in though, because I use that.

Mark: Yeah, that's correct. Yeah, it's not mandatory. They encourage it, though.

Participant: Now we have another software we use, which is Goldbar and I feel familiar with Goldbar, Zero and One, Mark Goldman's. His doesn't make it mandatory that you double opt in. Which is why we use AWeber instead for our autoresponders.

Mark: Well, you know why companies do it. They're trying to get their deliverability up to the major ISPs and if you've got people that are spamming off of their servers, that creates a lot of headaches for them. So the more that they can do the double opt-in thing to make sure that the customers of AWeber, or Mark's system Goldbar1, and that's a good system too, the more that they can assure the ISPs that they're trying. And that if one of their customers messes up, guess where you end up if you're that customer? You are out of there. You're out on the limb, they're the tree, they've got the chainsaw and zip! You're gone! Because they want to protect the relationship with the ISPs.

Participant: The question is why should I have a shopping cart versus PayPal or ClickBank, plus AWeber, or any of this?

Mark: By shopping cart what do you mean?

Participant: Shopping cart like Goldbar is a shopping cart.

Mark: Right. Or 1ShoppingCart.

Participant: Right. Or 1ShoppingCart, which you have to pay every month.

Mark: Yeah I wouldn't. I hate things where I have to pay every month.

Participant: So is there any benefit?

Participant: If you go through ClickBank or PayPal or something like that, you have a single transaction for each product, so you could wind up if you have two or three products from the same site that you wanted to purchase, you'd have three separate transactions that you have to go through. If you have a shopping cart you just put everything that you want into the shopping cart and one transaction would do it.

Mark: Right. And I can't remember if IDevAffiliate will do that for you or not. So if a real, live shopping cart where you can get multiple products in one transaction is important, you need to check that out.

Participant: And then, I get charged by the merchant account and buy the, I forgot what it's called that's in-between the merchant account and the shopping cart; the gateway. All these add up.

Mark: Yeah. PayPal is pretty easy. I mean, I've got a real full-blown merchant account and I do 99% of my stuff through PayPal at ClickBank.

So why? It's because in case my relationship with PayPal goes out, I've got another merchant account. You've got to manage your payment processors just like you manage all the other parts of your business.

So, Who's The Boss?

Okay, managing your business. Just because you have computers now, you've still got to make all of your business decisions. And even more so does it become evident, because if you're going solo entrepreneur Internet, you're the person. There are no other humans that are making decisions. If you have employees, you hire people to help make decisions on a second-tier management. They're in charge of doing things and making decisions on your behalf, and if they make the wrong decisions then you get rid of them, or manage them, or tell them what to do. If you are going solo, you are making all the decisions, you're setting up all the systems or buying into somebody else's system, like a 1ShoppingCart or whatever it is. You're buying their solution for that part of your marketing system, business system. So you've got to know what you want it to do, and lot of times those kinds of system work for you and sometimes they don't.

If you keep running into situations where you want to do something and the software doesn't allow it, you need to look for a different system. Because there will be something else out there which is more flexible.

Participant: You had mentioned AWeber. We do use AWeber and we like it too, but therefore you're saying that all the time it's better to use a third party than to have your own software on your server?

Mark: No. I don't like third party. I like to have my stuff on my own server.

Participant: Yeah, that's what I thought. Because first of all, the mail goes out fast, you don't have to worry about other people; you only have to worry about your own responsibility.

Mark: Right! If I screw up, I deserve it. Okay, the problem is that

I'm not a bad guy but I am still having deliverability problems because of these ISPs. So I had to, like a lot of the stuff that AWeber does in developing relationships with the larger ISPs, I have to do that myself.

It's worth it to me, because then I don't have AWeber telling me how to do business. If I want to send out a special thank-you e-mail, I don't have to get AWeber to approve it. I make my own decisions. So for me, I like to be able to communicate directly to the customer the best I can, with nobody telling me what I can and can't do. On the other hand, I take the full responsibility for that.

Participant: So is there any downside to get the software rather than to use a service like AWeber?

Mark: The only downside is deliverability. Now somebody like AWeber says that they've got great deliverability. I don't know.

For myself, I've got to work on MSN and Hotmail, and it seems to me that there's one other ISP that I'm still having trouble with. But they've got a whole different system. They use something call BrightMail to filter things. I just haven't had the time to try to work on that one yet.

Now the other thing is, it's just as easy to go into my system and say, "I don't take MSN subscribers," and that takes care of that. Of course, I get people writing to me and asking, "Why not?" They just don't understand the headaches these ISPs are doing.

AOL, that's a whole different story. See, we talked about Yahoo a second ago. AOL has got their own thing. So I have been through the loop with them, too. They had a particular thing, and here's the cute thing about AOL. You can actually sign up for a service there, then if somebody puts you in their spam box AOL will notify you. Now the useful thing would be to do what? That they would actually send you that persons e-mail address, so you could get them out of your database, right? No, they don't do that. They send you back your own e-mail.

Now the good news is, in the bottom of all my e-mails I've got un-subscribe links, so I can get the un-subscribe link like that person should have done to begin with, and I can go unsubscribe them that way. But the first time I started seeing that, I thought, "Well what good is this? They send the e-mail back to you. So what? There are only I don't know how many thousands of people at AOL that are subscribers. How am I going to figure this out?"

Then I saw that I could open up the thing and get the link and get rid of them. I've also got a thing where I can click it and see exactly who did it, what their e-mail address is and everything like that. The temptation, of course, is to write them and let them have it. Get over that really quick, okay? It's not worth it. Just delete him and you're on your way.

By the way, if somebody e-mails you back and uses big capital letters and nasty words, you just got a nasty gram. The best thing to do is not answer it, do not flame back the other way, you just get them out of your database and move on. I know you're approaching your business that you want to help people, but you will get hold of some people that are just nasty. They turn around and they just unload on you. It's going to make you feel real lousy when that happens because you'll take it personally; because you care.

But just take a deep breath, put your hand on all the words and the names they're calling you, get their e-mail address and delete it from your database and be on with it. [Laughter]

Okay?

How To Find Groups Of People That Are Already Interested In What You Offer

What else?

Finding people. Early on, when I started marketing online, the best places to start finding people were in forums and newsgroups, and I think it still is. I mean it's the cheap way. Think about this just for a second. If you've got more time than money you will have to do more work, so you're going to have to go looking for what? The ponds.

So now we're coming back to where I was, we are back to the ponds. Where are the ponds on the Internet? The forums, the newsgroups, the big Web sites where people hang out and congregate. That's where you need to be spending your time to find people who are like-minded. Okay?

This is the herd mentality. People travel in groups, right? Y'all are here. Why? You have a common interest. Here we have a herd.

Friday night down at the brickyard; last night at a ball game. What were those people into? Baseball. Okay? That's a herd.

Shopping malls across the street, what are they into? Shopping. That's a herd. So you want to hang out where the herd hangs out.

The cool thing is, you get to see the questions they're asking, you get to see the answers that are being given, you actually get to see who the other experts are, or who have already established themselves as experts. You can start developing your relationships.

One of the things you absolutely should do is use your real name when you are posting in a forum. Why do you think you might want to do that? Yeah, you want to brand yourself as somebody who is helpful and positive and useful-and expert status.

Now when you first go into a forum, do you start giving everybody advice and telling everybody what to do?

No.

Yeah, some do. Then what happens? They get shot down and they go down in blazes, right?

So get in there and see what the rules are; the unwritten rules of the forum. What's the tone, how do people respond? With positive, negative, or in the middle. Whatever it is. Who's already recognized as an expert. You don't want to go toe-to-toe with them, right? Because they already have a following there at the forum, or the newsgroup, or wherever you're plugged in. Bulletin board systems, wherever it is.

So come in there and add to discussions that are going, and one of the smart things you could do is, this person who maybe is already recognized as an expert, maybe the first thing out of your finger tips is, and what Bill said is right on the money. In other words, agree with them and build up whatever their comment was.

Just set your ego off to the side for a moment so that it's okay to do this, and then you add on top of it to emphasize the point, or add a little experience that you've had along the same lines.

So that's going to position you as a nice, helpful person who is non-threatening to somebody who is already there.

Remember, glance, smile, conversation, cup of coffee, lunch, movie, dinner. It progresses; baby steps.

If ever, ever, ever you run into a situation where you are getting resistance from the other person, back up and create at least three baby steps out of the leap that you asked them to do.

Participant: If you are going after a market in which you are not an expert, but you see the potential and you see the need, et cetera. And you start hitting these forums to start what you're talking about; building those relationships. What is your advice to really connecting with this group of people when you really are not really one of them? You just want to meet their need and you know you have a sort of hidden agenda. But how do you really kind of establish yourself as an "expert" when you don't have that history?

Mark: Okay, I mean to make posts where you're giving advice, you do have to have some expertise. Now you can acquire that expertise very quickly by reading a lot and doing research. The other thing that you are going to spot in the forums, if you're sharp, and you are, is that you're going to see what other people type. The lingo and the language they use; what terms that they use. When you answer, you're going to use that same terminology, so that you are one of them. Because it's really easy to spot somebody who is trying to mooch off of the marketplace.

You're going to have to speak their language. That's why I keep going back into really understanding the emotions in the marketplace. Like in this ISS system, the first three sessions are all about the marketplace and the competition. That six hours of audio and hundreds of pages; and recommended reading on the topic that most people have read it, but they didn't really get out of it what they were supposed to when they read it.

So you can see how much I put on this, that if you don't get this part right, the rest of it doesn't matter, because you're gonna be seen as an outsider and nobody wants you.

How Can You Sell Information If You're Not The Expert

Participant: If your competitor, let's say you're going after car mechanics. You have never even changed a spark plug, have no idea how to change oil, and you go to the forum because you want to write an e-book on CarMechanicsSecrets.com and you've figured out that they have a need. The competitors that may have some products that are not really as comprehensive, they all have a history, they all are car mechanics.

So I guess my question comes down to establishing your credibility with this market. Do you kind of come at it with, "I'm the non-mechanic car mechanic expert"?

I mean, how do you hit it when you really don't have the credentials, I guess.

Mark: Okay, or you go find yourself a car mechanic expert and you be the marketer. That's going to be the easier way to go because the car mechanic may not know the marketing side of things and what a joint venture that could be.

They get to be the car mechanic, and you get to go in there and use their name, to where you are just doing the stuff to get it done.

That's the way I would approach it. It's a lot harder for you to slide in there and position yourself as a car mechanic if you've been a car mechanic for like three days. You don't have enough grease underneath your fingernails and nobody is going to look at you.

[Laughter]

Participant: I think that's a real important point. With some of these groups, I mean there's a barrier there. Like a car mechanic or an electrical engineer, I mean unless you have that expertise and you talk their talk and stuff like that, I don't think you are going to gain admittance, or whatever, to that group. So what you said, finding the car mechanic and then doing the marketing, I mean you're beating your head against the wall a lot less by going that route than you are trying to establish yourself as an expert to that group.

Mark: Yeah. It depends on what service or product you're going to offer to the marketplace, also. If I came into the, my brother is an electrical engineer so I am not going to go there, I will go someplace else. [Laughter]

Car mechanics. It depends on what I am going to offer to the car mechanics. If I was going to offer car mechanics great ways to increase their business, then 80% of what I've got to say is what I could say to any other business. I would customize the other 20% to car mechanics. Yeah, it would be great to have a couple of car mechanics who I've done this for as testimonials, where they could come in and say, "Yeah, this guy's not a car mechanic but he doesn't need to be. He knows how to jack up the profits instead of the back-end of the car."

That's the value that I am bringing to the car mechanic forum, is how to make more money from your car repair shop. Whereas the other guys are teaching them how to do the nuts and bolts; I'm saying, "Okay, let me show you how to get more customers so you can do the nuts and bolts."

So it depends on what you're going to offer them. But even so, I need to talk car mechanics, with the kind of language they would use, whatever that is. So that I have empathy and they can spot it, that I know where they live and what their experience is and what they're up against.

Participant: Yeah, I just wanted to add, that's one other aspect of it is, in addition to being the marketing arm for this car mechanic, you could also start to brand yourself as the person who knows how to translate the technical jargon of the mechanic into the layman's terms.

Mark: Um hmm.

Steve?

Participant: Say I want to have a bunch of different niches, say dog training, relationships, car mechanics, and so forth. If the market looks worthy I want to go all the way up to producing a product, ultimately, and I don't want to learn everything that much about those things. But I want to have this, sort of like the politician has the little thing in his ear and he's saying, "Should that person that I select from the forum or from some other place, should that person be the public face, or should that still be me?"

In another words, should he be the person who is the front person for that, or should I be that person? Because I am interested in outsourcing the whole thing and in just sort of being the Wizard of Oz guy who does the plumbing and makes the thing work for different markets. Can you speak to that a little bit, please?

Mark: Yeah, it's going to go one way or the other, and it's probably how good a chameleon you are. Now would I believe that you're an expert car mechanic? If we had a whole bunch of car mechanics showing up here this weekend and we're going to talk about making your car mechanic shop work great; if you got up and talked and just your years of being Steve, are you going to fit in as a car mechanic guy? Umm, not a chance. And that's okay.

But if you had the car mechanic specialist who ran a shop, who was in the top 1% of all car repair shops in the country, and knew how to turn these things. Not only did he do it in one car shop but he has done in 15 counties around where he lives, and you are the guy who helped him do it and showed him how to do it. He's up there first and he introduces you as the guy who can pull this off, how are all the car mechanics sitting in the audience going to view you as you walk up to talk to them? They're going to applaud, right? They are going to love you, and you are one of them just because you were endorsed by the big superhero mechanic in the business.

So it's going to be more of a joint venture situation.

How Do You Structure The Business Relationships, The Profits, And The Money Aspect Of Joint Ventures?

Participant: I think your last statement leads in really nicely to my next question on JVs. When you are joint venturing with experts in these niche markets, where they are not marketers per se, that scenario. Would you talk about how you structure the business relationships, the profits, the money aspect, the changing of hands. Obviously we have all this Internet online marketing salesmanship stuff, whereas they think, "I am just a car mechanic, I don't know anything else." How can you build into this kind of profit potential, where you're not maybe giving away too much of the pie. Just how would you do it, and kind of talking about the language of the written documents.

Mark: Okay. It may not surprise you; it's all negotiable. It just depends on where you're positioned in the relationship. Have you done this in other industries, have you done it in that industry, who have you done it for? Are you endorsed by those people to this other person?

After that it could come down to 50/50. You are bringing the marketing expertise, they're bringing the expert expertise to the thing. You are picking their brains so you do have something to market. That's 50/50 on getting the thing to show to the public.

Now there are other issues, too, such as infrastructure. This person has no infrastructure and let's start there. If you are going to have to put more into it on the infrastructure side, that may weigh things more in your direction. It just depends on how badly you want to deal, because where you will get eventually with this is that you will cherry pick your projects. Because you will know how to turn these situations into money for yourself and other people, and that's a real valuable talent as a marketer. Because in any marketplace you can go into the marketplace, and sometimes it can take you longer than others because you don't have the background. But if you've got the right mindset of what I've been talking about this morning, you can go into any marketplace and sit on the side of the table of the customer and be advocate for the customer.

You very, very quickly, by you asking them or other strategies such as that, will be able to pick up on what the frustrations are in the marketplace; the hopes, dreams, doubts, fears. All that kind of stuff; more so than people who've been in the market for 20 or 30 or 40 years.

There's a guy, back in my hometown I did a thing for the Chamber of Commerce. This goes back a few years, and we had about 20 people sitting in a room, they were all business owners, local business people. It was a Mayberry, RFD kind of town, right? There was one, the youngest guy ran a car shop, a repair shop. So it's interesting, all this conversation. I was thinking of him.

We went around the room and what I asked people to do was write down, of the business that person is in, the rest in the room write down what their biggest complaint was about that industry.

Now you can imagine a car repair shop. How many of you love going to your car repair shop? Okay, there is one out of a bunch. And it was the same thing that night. We sat around and he heard from the other 19 people everything that they hated about the car repair industry, and instead of taking it personally, he wrote everything down. Because he had a whole bunch of business people, smart people, time was important to them, they knew business and they were telling him exactly what they didn't like about his industry.

"You walk in, it's grimy and greasy, you feel like you are getting dirty as soon as you open the door, there are various kinds of calendars hanging all over the wall in various car shops."

[Laughter]

It was a certain way that car shops many times are. So he took all this, he took pages and pages of notes, and three months later he had completely painted the outside of his car repair shop like this bright blue color with yellow. I mean it just looked spotless. If you go down the street, if you'd seen this drab building, it just sparkled now. He cleaned up all the oil out of way, and all that kind of stuff. He, instead of working on any cars at all, sat there behind the desk and worked the phone and computer. He ran the business.

Every time a customer was in there, he was there to shake hands and smile at them and call by name. When he had his computer set up to where when you call him and give him your name, he'd be talking to you and chatting, he'd get the name first while you are chatting, he'd be typing in your last name, boom, boom, boom. He'd ask, "Is that the Chrysler or the Chevy?" He had all the data there. I mean he was like talking about your children. He was that good. This guy really snapped to it. He increased the profits of that business in three months, incredibly.

They were always booked, and he worked it for couple of years and it was his parents' place. He turned that business around. I talked to him a year or two later and he said, "Yeah, I am kind of getting bored with this, because there really is no upside to this place." Then I noticed that he had left, and you know what happened to business? It went down. They sold the business to somebody else and within about six months the place was out of business. And the joint was jumping when he was managing it that way.

He was on the customers' side of things and the customers responded. That's all it took, was listening to the customers and taking action on it, not just lip-service but actually doing what the customer wants. The customers will tell you exactly what they want.

They are the marketing experts. Think of it that way. If you'll just listen to them, they're the experts telling you exactly what they want. Don't fight them; just do it.

Seven Things To Do To Market On A Shoestring Budget

Participant: Mark if you had an information product that you wanted to market on a shoestring budget of less than $25, can you give me seven things that you would do?

Mark: Yeah. I would hit the forums and news groups to develop rapport and show expertise. In the little resource box where you usually have links or something, you can make a little listing thing, right? Yeah, signature box, thanks. Instead of talking about yourself, make an offer for a special, free report that they would find interesting. This all comes back to list building.

See, list building is all about relationships. Like with Steve, he was at that thing in Orlando last week, and all we talked about was that list building is relationships; making friends. So you are going to offer them something of value that they would value even more than giving up their name and e-mail address to you, and permission for you to contact them thereafter. That's the first step.

Now how much does it cost you to do that? Nothing!

You can go to PRWeb or any of those public release sites, and at PRWeb you can post public releases for free. Those get out and they stay there and people pick up on them. You've got to get good at writing press releases. They have a whole team there that will review things for you, and they've got a lot of educational materials. One of the things you've got to remember about press releases is you cannot write about yourself. You have to write like it's a newspaper writer.

Participant: And they have directions on the right side and I wrote a press release and I got an e-mail saying it was rated number four.

I said, "What's four?"

"Well, five is a best read. I don't give many fives."

I said, "How did I do that?"

He said, "You followed the questions."

I said, "Well, doesn't everybody?"

[Laughter]

Mark: No!

Participant: He said, "Very few people do."

Mark: Right. Yeah, most people have their ego and they want to talk about themselves instead of writing it from a reporter situation.

Participant: And if you get used to it and you get good, you could do a press release every other day. And the more press releases, the more Google picks you up.

Mark: That's right! Then go to article directories, and here's one you can go to. UltimateArticleDirectory.com. Who do you think might own that?

www.UltimateArticleDirectory.com You can post quality articles. Don't post any junk there; not that you would. You can get link-backs to your site and people go there and grab articles, and they publish them and they stick them in their books and on their pages and all kinds of stuff.

The other tip that I will give you, their software, and there's even a software thing that I've got there for sale. But I'll tell you, the best thing you can do is go to the top ten article sites and if you go to whatever your favorite search engine is and type in "article directory" and poke around, and if you look by Alexa numbers and stuff like that, you will find the top ten sites. I've got a list of them that I gave to the list group last week.

Anyway, that's what you can do. Post to those top ten and don't worry about the other 990, because the search engines are already showing up there to find those articles and then you'll get link-backs to your place. I had one that I posted just a week or two ago, I guess two weeks ago it was, and when I searched for the title of it, I was already seeing like 500 or more places where it showed up on the Web sites. It happens that quick, where people pick it up and post it and grab it and stick it in for their own content.

Participant: And about articles, people think, "Wow, I have to be writer." It's not as difficult as people would think.

Mark: Right. I showed a trick to the list building group last week and Louis Burleson is an ISS member; he is a sharp marketer in his own right. He quickly got the idea of what I was talking about. One of the exercises we did was to go out and find 12 articles, and you are going to use that for the basis of a PDF e-book, and that's going to be your freebie. You are going to use 12 articles by somebody else; your name's going to be on the cover, and you are going to give credit to them in the little resource boxes. You're going to have a table of contents and you are not going to mention anybody's name until the resource box.

It's going to be organized in some kind of chapter where it makes sense, the articles. You're going to take enough time to put it in the logical order to where the people can follow along the topic.

But you're going to find 12 great articles, compile it into a PDF e-book, give it a title; the whole thing. If you have some artwork to make it look pretty, that would add value to it. It will be by you.

It establishes you as what? An expert. And guess what you are also going to use these articles for? You've got an autoresponder, right? When they sign up you are going to load these articles into your autoresponder. There's your sequence over the next whatever, 12 weeks, whatever you want it to be. You're actually going to add a little intro to it, add a little actionable content and a little summary, and lead them to go look at something else that they can maybe buy. Or maybe some other freebie that they would want to get.

So you can take other people's content and make actionable content out of it, and position yourself as an expert all at once.

Does this help at all?

Okay, that's maybe three or four out of seven. Keep it coming, right?

[Laughter]

Aw, you're trying to sneak ten out of me, and you only said seven!

Participant: If you call repackaging your own articles that you're going to write, that counts as another one?

Mark: Okay, you could do 5,6,7

[Laughter]

Yeah, I mean you can grab articles from other people and rewrite them, and that way you don't include anybody's name on the thing, other than yours.

Now when you rewrite them put them in your own tone, and you will agree or not agree per paragraph or sentence with the person.

How quickly can you establish your expertise if you went out and found 12 great articles on a particular topic, and rewrote them in your own tone of voice?

Now the depth of your expertise could be questioned, so would you want to get up in front of a crowd of people and talk for three days at this stage of game? Probably not. But I'll tell you what, if you kept this research up, in six months you could because you'd know more about it than 99% of all the other people you probably would have met in six months.

If you really went after this, you probably would have met or hosted on a teleseminar, or done some kind of a joint relationship with experts in that field. Maybe you couldn't stand up and talk for three days, but how about if you organized the conference and you hosted the conference?

By the way if you host a conference, does that establish you as an expert in that field? Very quickly; which you might want to do. If you can get people to show up, and you may not be able to do this with the superheroes, the As. But you might be able to put together one with the Bs, where they market to their lists and they're driving people to the conference, and you are the host. You put the deal together. That's a real quick way to establish yourself as the person.

I would start doing them again if you are trying to get into info products and that kind of business.

Someone else had a question I think, right?

Mark: Did we get the seventh?

Participant: Yeah.

Mark: I can't even remember what the seven were.

Participant: How about one more? A bonus!

Okay the seven were: 1) Going to forums, 2) PRWeb, 3) Article directories, 4) Top 10 article sites, 3 and 4 are kind of one merged together, 5)Rewriting someone else's articles, 6) writing your own.

Mark: How many is that?

Participant: Six!

Mark: What was the question?

Participant: The question is if you had an information product to market and you were on a shoestring budget of $25 or less, what are seven things you would do?

Mark: The seventh one would be to do all those, and when they got there to get their freebie. Immediately after they get their freebie, give them the chance to buy the book at a discount.

Participant: Upsell!

Mark: Upsell the freebie to a purchase.

Participant: See, now I've got a bonus because I didn't count events; do a live event

Mark: There you go. Okay.

How To Generate Content Easily And Quickly

Participant: When you were at the beginning you were talking about gathering articles. These are articles that you put in the book and you give credit to the person you are finding the article from? On that page you're giving them credit because you found their article, right? But then you are also saying to rewrite the articles? Which I am sure I can do.

Mark: Yeah, you can do that also, and that way you don't have to give credit to anybody.

Participant: I'm a writer, so I can probably do that.

Mark: I mean how much really new stuff is under the sun?

Participant: Well, I write about raw foods, so we have a select group of writers. They might know I am stealing from them. [Laughter] But I'll find a way of working on it.

Mark: Yeah, I mean you've got your own ways to phrases thing, right?

Participant: Yeah. Okay, cool.

Mark: You're basically do a research on what somebody else has said, and if I go find 12 articles on things and I put them all together and toss it up and then I rephrase it the way I would tell people, then it becomes me. And that's me, not them, right? That's what writing is all about.

I mean all the great symphonies are all built on the same 12 notes, if you think about that. It's all re-ordering and putting things in different places and having different instruments play it and stuff like that, but it's really all based on the 12 same notes.

Okay. Why don't we take a lunch break?

Using Articles To Create A Book To Use As A Lead Generator

- Audio Three Transcript –

The listbuilding workshop information can be found at:

www.GrandmasterOfListbuilding.com

Mark: All right, let me show you a little bit about what can be done pretty, pretty quick as far these 12 articles and putting it into a PDF book form and setting up a simple little page to capture e-mail addresses and send people over to an affiliate program.

Here's the one I mentioned. Louis Burleson is an ISS member; he was at the List Building Conference last week down in Orlando and in a matter of a few hours he put this all together. The assignment was to find 12 articles, put it into a PDF book and then put together a little Web site with a subscription form tied into your autoresponder system, get them to a thank-you page where they can download the thing, and make them an offer of something else. That was the idea. Then start driving traffic through it. So that's what we did during that weekend.

So the first thing he did was to put together his e-book. Now Louis is pretty good at graphics stuff; I mean not heavy graphics but he went and found a picture of a golf driver and a ball on a T. Then he puts some color on the top and he came up with a little headline, "How to Play Better Gold by This Weekend: The Quick and Easy Way to Lower Your Gold Score Without Spending a Dime. 12 Incredible, Simple Golf Tips You Can Use Today to Shave Strokes Off Your Score Tomorrow."

How about that! Twelve! Incredible. [Laughter] Now we know what those might be, right? Those are the 12 articles he found. He's got a little covering letter inside; it's from him. Right off the bat, he's got a recommended resource. Why do we put the recommended resource right up at the front of the book instead of the end of the book?

Right. He wants to get paid. Has anybody ever bought a book that you didn't get to the end of the book? Yeah, all of us. Okay? So if we're going to sell something, why don't we put the offer right up front because people will at least read it that far, right?

Now he's also got it at the end of the book, but I told him, "You need to put your offers right up at the front."

So he signed up for an affiliate program, and you click here and it gets you over to that. So it's going to continue. Okay, he's even got a table of contents so you can read about what's coming up. It's all these great headlines; headlines get people interested so they will read stuff, right?

So now we've got all these things in a particular order that he reordered after getting these articles. And there's Chapter One. You notice he doesn't call it Article One? He calls it a Chapter. So what's more valuable, a chapter or an article? Chapters. Even though they're articles, we call them chapters.

He gives credit to the author there, if you go through it, doesn't it look nice? It looks like something of value. Then he's got information about the author who actually wrote the article.

You'll notice that he did not put clickable links in it. Why do we not want to put clickable links in it?

Yeah, because they'll click on it and there they go.

Why?

I gave them your e-mail or your Web site address. I gave you full credit and how to get in touch with you. Who said that I had to make my links clickable?

Now on a Web site would that be nice to do for somebody?

Yeah.

Is this against the law?

No.

Chapter two, next guy, and on and on and on. So the layout is nice and clean; chapter 3. So all told it's 29 pages of a valuable book for golfers on how to shave strokes off the game before whatever the benefit was, right?

Use today to shave strokes off your score tomorrow.

So that's the bait.

Now a topic came up at lunch, and it was, "Gosh, don't I have to be a great copywriter to do this kind of stuff?"

And the answer is, "No!"

You see how many pages this stuff is for this? That's it.

What did he do? He writes a little personal letter with a good headline and a sub-headline and he talks to them a little bit. "Dear fellow golf fanatic."

Why does he say that? He wants to imply that I am one of you guys. "Dear fellow golf fanatic."

He talks about being crazy about golf and how much he spends on golf just to try to shave a stroke off your score, and stuff like that. And on and on and on.

Then he introduces the product, of which this is a free product.

Now you notice that he goes to all the trouble to sell a free product. There is a transaction happening on this page.

What's the transaction?

The e-mail address and the first name.

Folks, there is always a transaction in every communication that you do. You are always selling something. You are selling your ideas, your opinion on a certain matter, communicating that to somebody else, and they're either buying it or they're not. Right?

In every conversation you have, they're either buying what you say or not. There is some kind of transaction happening.

So now he has introduced the product, which is this e-book, and he is going to include 3,5,6,7 whatever it is, major benefits of that book and instead of saying, "And much, much more," he says, "And that's just the tip of the iceberg."

It's just different ways of saying the same thing.

He tells them what they simply have to do and they get the copy of this and they fill it in. Send the e-book report now.

He assures them it's for his purpose only, privacy is assured and this kind of stuff.

Signs off personally: "Louis."

All right, now we go over to after they sign up here's a simple little page. Here's where they click to get it, here's the information sent via e-mail and while you are at it, here's the recommended resources.

If you are into golf that much, you might also be interested in this. Have you noticed that Amazon does this to you all the time when you buy a book at Amazon? They recommend like two or three things right off the bat, bang!

And they try to upsell you. If you buy $25 worth, or something like that, you get free shipping. So if you bundle you save a couple of bucks on the shipping cost. Now of course that's regular delivery, and I don't know about you, but most of the time if I am looking for something in Amazon I usually get it shipped quicker than regular delivery.

So even if I bundle up it's not an issue. But it gets you going, doesn't it?

Participant: One thing I see from his site here, on the thank-you page, I assume this is where they go right after they hit

Mark: I can't remember if he makes them go to e-mail or not, yeah.

Participant: Because if that's the case they haven't opted into his list yet.

Mark: I don't remember if he did that or not.

I showed people six different ways to do Internet plumbing, just on setting up name capture pages like this. Depending on whether you wanted to send them to a double opt-in page or one-time offers, and all of these variations of that.

If they took the one-time offer, what happens after that? So there is all this plumbing that I showed people last week on how to do this kind of stuff,. Would you like to see one or two of those?

Now it's not fair to them if I show you them all, okay? Sorry.

MARK HENDRICKS

Autoresponder Plumbing – How To Get Your Subscribers Through Your System

Here is, I call it plumbing; autoresponder plumbing. Here is the first simple example; you have a subscribe page and the person gets to a thank-you page or a download page, and he gets the first e-mail sent out by the system.

So everything in the top part is what the visitor sees. The things down here in the bottom line, connected by the dotted lines, are what's happening behind-the-scenes by the autoresponder system.

So they get to the subscribe page, telling them about what you are going to give them, and there is the subscription order form. They click the submit button. The next thing that happens is that information gets sent to the autoresponder system for the name capture. It gets stuck in the database and the system sends them to the downward page, the thank-you download page, and at the same time sends them the first e-mail message.

That's the simplest way to do it.

The second way is a subscription form. They fill in their information, that information goes to the autoresponder system, from the name capture to the database, and then the system sends out the first e-mail message, which would include the download link. And they would get that from the e-mail message, and then you would send them to the thank-you page.

Now why would you use this instead of the other?

Right, because in case somebody sends you a junk e-mail that they never ever check, we're going to let them know that you're going to get the download address by way of the e-mail that the system is going to send you.

So they put in their name and address, and let's say that they use a bogus address. The system gets it and sends them out an e-mail message with the download link in it, the address of this page. It's going to send them out an e-mail message with the download thank-you page address in it, but guess what?

It was a bum address. They don't get the goodie.

Once they figure this out they back up and go to the subscription page, and they will use their real e-mail address.

Participant: So in this second method then, when you have your code in your opt-in box in the form that normally you put a redirect page, just leave that blank? There would be no redirect page? Do you know what I'm saying?

Like when you have the code in your opt-in box, normally there is a redirect page which on your first model there would be the page that they will go to without having to open their e-mail. This one would be left blank? You'd put no redirect there?

Mark: Oh, you'd have a page that says, "Thanks! Go check your e-mail. "

Sorry I think I left that off this box. Yes, that ought to be there.

There should actually be another box up here, where there is a page that says, "Thanks for subscribing. Go check your e-mail." Then they get the e-mail and they get the thank-you page.

That's right. I forgot that stuff.

How about another one? I'll do four of these.

Here is one where we have an opt-in. They are at the subscribe page, they put in their name and address, it goes to the AR system, AR system sends them out and once again says, "Thank you. Go check your e-mail."

Right?

It sends them the opt-in e-mail message, they click it to confirm, it goes to the AR system, at that time it sends them to the thank-you download page and their first e-mail message, which is relating to something else.

So everything up here is what the people see. Here's what's going on in the background. Here they see the first e-mail message, too.

The fourth one is that we add a one-time offer, and this is not double opt-in, okay? On the subscribe page they put in their information that goes to the AR system, it delivers them to a one-time offer, in other words upsell. You gave them something free, now you're going to offer them something right then to buy if they would like.

Of course they have a yes or no, so if it's yes it goes over to your order processing download pages and goes through all that plumbing.

If they say no, then they are going to go to the thank-you page and download the freebie. Then the AR system is sending out the first e-mail in the midst of all this stuff.

Okay?

So the big mistake that people make when you try to organize this stuff is if you go into your autoresponder system and you're trying to do this inside the system.

I would suggest that just like I have got boxes with arrows and things, go get a sheet of paper and a pen, and draw pictures so that you can see it on one piece of paper.

Then go inside your autoresponder system and make it happen inside there.

Okay? That's because most people get really confused inside of an autoresponder system, until you get experienced. Then you will be very comfortable. But as it gets more complicated, like the five, six, and seven examples here that I gave to everybody, I mean, I write stuff on paper.

I've been doing it for years and when it starts where you get all these if-thens; if they do this and that and the other, and you get two different offers on the upside. You may have a basic package one-time offer, but you have the premium package, too.

So depending on which one they choose they go a different direction, and you've got to tie all this back together and make sure that they get their freebie, too.

So it can get confusing and that's why I say draw it out on paper, get the flow correct, and then do it in your autoresponder system. Okay?

Has that been helpful, to understand autoresponders a little bit?

Should One-Time-Offers Really Be Only Offered One Time?

Lou?

Participant: Yeah, I just wanted to know if you could give your opinion on something. With the one-time offer upsell option, do you think there is any real difference, positive or negative, to attaching a cookie to that to where it truly is a one-time offer versus well, they can come back through again and get that one-time offer a second time?

Mark: Yeah, I have got a heavy big-time opinion on that. Remember that know you, like you, trust you stuff? If you tell somebody it's a one-time offer, then it had better be a one-time offer. Otherwise you just blew all your credibility.

Now if you're not going to do the little script that sets the cookie so that it will not show them that page, you can tell them that it's a special offer that they can take advantage of today. There is no guarantee that this page will be here tomorrow.

Now I have not said it's a one-time offer, but I have created scarcity. Okay?

Then every once in awhile you need to take those pages down, so the people can come back and see that they're gone.

So there are different ways to say it, but absolutely if you say something is going to expire at a certain time, or if you are going to only sell so many copies of something, or if it's a one-time offer, you better be telling the truth!

I don't know how well you all know me, but have you noticed that if I say something is expiring at 10 o'clock A.M. Eastern USA time on Tuesday morning, June 27th, if you show up at 10 o'clock you are going to see a different page. That's because at 9:59:58 my finger goes click, and it takes a couple of seconds for it to go.

Yes, sir.

Participant: One thing you might want to do with a one-time offer is to set it up so the page can't be downloaded. Because I was curious to see if this could work and I had a one-time offer that was going to expire once I left the page. I thought, "Let me see what happens," and I downloaded the page to my desktop and sure enough, the next day I went back and it was still there. It was on my desktop and I clicked the link to see if it still worked.

I could have bought it if I had wanted to. I don't know how many people would think to do that, but there might be a way to make a site so it can't be downloaded so people can't get around it.

Mark: Yeah, I see a lot of people doing that. The way I get around it as the seller, is that I rarely have a link that goes from the page directly to the order system. I have it go through a redirect where it's going through another file. The long order link stuff is inside that redirect file, so that if that thing expires I just rename that file and you can't get any place. You can click all day long and you're not getting to the deal.

Or I may have it set up to where at a certain time it reverts back to the regular price and even if somebody has the special page, if they click that link they are going to see the newer price.

So yeah, people are sneaky that way. Like you.

[Laughter]

What Kind Of Redirect Service Should You Use

Participant: So you are using like a TinyURL for those redirects?

Mark: No, if you go to Hunteridge.com - write this down-there is a free redirect script.

Hunteridge.com/redirect.txt - That's the extension, that's what I mean, and that's got instructions at the top. I think it's got like a dotted line, yeah.

Instructions here at the top; that's all this stuff. So what you would do is copy all this starting with the opening HTML to the closing HTML. Go paste that in another file and do it in Notepad. Do not do it in Microsoft Word or any software like that.

Do it in Notepad and what you will do is, where you want them sent, you will put the full URL address, the Web site address, right there. Where it says, "Insert affiliate address here," or whatever address you want to use.

If you're going to an affiliate sales page, you can go there first and find out what they put, the words they put in that very, very top blue bar in a browser. The very top of your screen; the blue one.

Grab the title and you put in the title of the page right here, where it says, "Insert the title of your page here."

If you wanted to do keywords and stuff like that, you could. I don't really bother.

Then you save that file as something that relates to the product or not, depending on if you want to give people a hint on what it's about.

You could say "saveongolfstrokes.html" or .htm, however you want to do your extensions

Or if you wanted to be not so blatant, you could have it to be sogs.htm, right? "Save On Golf Strokes."

In that, once you give people the address, it would be yourdomain.com/sogs.htm, and that would redirect them through that file on your server to the address that you put in the URL address right there.

Does everybody followed?

That would be your affiliate link right here. "Insert affiliate address here."

So on the way from your domain, your Web site, going through this sogs.htm, file the affiliate cookie is set on the way over and they then end up on the person's Web site, the sales site, and your cookie is set.

Any questions?

Go ahead.

Participant: There are a couple of different ways to do the redirect page, of course. Why would you name the title of the page? They don't ever actually see that.

Mark: Yeah, they do.

Participant: Oh, they do?

Mark: Flowing through the redirect, it takes a second or two.

Participant: Oh! It still shows the page and the URL address in the window, the difference is it is showing the page that you're redirecting through.

Mark: This little blue bar here at the top shows, and when you click on this sogs.htm, at the very top it will say, "Save On Golf Strokes," and that should match up.

So this is called congruency, right? That whatever the little title bar at the very top says, I like to see that match up with the sales page at the top, also.

Little stuff does matter, because people get real funny about affiliate links. You all are really nice. I was kind of kidding around and I was giving you your choice. You can go directly to the site or here's my affiliate link.

That puts the ball in your court. You get to make a choice.

Some people will go direct and some people will buy through my affiliate link. I don't know which one you'll choose, but I'll give you both options.

Now the other one that you didn't use is a piece of software and it costs money. Here's a free way to do it that I just gave you.

Okay?

One of the things that ISS members know me for is that if I know a free way to do it, I'll give them the free way. Typically it will take you more time because it's free, right? You have to spend more time.

If you've got a little bit of money and less time, most of the time it's better to go ahead and buy software that does stuff.

So this is one that does stuff. It's www.Market-Soft.com/redirector

Now on that page, once you get to it and look at it, there are actually two redirectors. There is the redirector, which is exactly this, except there's a software form where you fill-in-the-blanks and press a button and it does the stuff for you. You save the file and you upload it and you're done.

There is another one called "redirector plus" which is the stealth version of this thing, to where the people will never, ever see that you have set cookies on their computer and you can redirect them to different pages, other than where the normal affiliate link would send them.

For instance, if somebody is running some kind of promotion and their sales pages is nothing more than a squeeze page.

Do we all know what that means? It's a horrible name for what it is. [Laughter]

But it squeezes the person's name and address out of them before you let them go to see what else there is. It's basically a name capture page, so it's all the benefits given to them before they even get a chance to be sold.

How about that? So your affiliate link would get to a page like that, which is no more than a screen that talks about the main benefits about what they are about to learn. But they have to give up their name and e-mail address just to read about the thing. Not to get it, just to read about it.

Now if I don't want to send all my readers over there to join that person's mailing list for nothing, I can use my stealth redirector, and in 99% of the cases, you've got to check things and make sure it works right. But I can send them to the real sales page and never have to have them sign up for an e-mail list.

Now if they become a customer is it okay with me that they would have them on their list?

Absolutely.

But like in joint ventures that I do, I mean the major joint ventures that you see, I never, ever will send any of my people to a squeeze page just to read somebody else's sales page.

Never.

The visitor feels manipulated by that, too. Now the reason it's done is it creates a hoop that people have to jump through, which if people are willing to jump through that hoop, they are willing to follow directions. So it's absolutely a psychological trick.

Okay?

It plays on that, that once a person takes that baby step, they're more willing to take the next step. That's why it works.

Okay, so that's redirects.

There are a few different ways to do them. You can do them with PHP scripts and stuff like that. Java scripts; you can do them with Java scripts. This is like the real, simple, easy way to do it.

I've had other guys who knew a lot fancier programming than me who've seen this, and they go, "I didn't know you could do it that way!" And they converted over to doing it this way because it's cleaner and more simple.

Java script sometimes gets blocked by people's browsers and stuff like that, and PHP for some people is more challenging to kind of learn that language just a little bit.

Anyway, so this works.

MARK HENDRICKS

Sales Copywriting Secrets You Need To Know

Mark: What else were we talking about?

Copywriting.

Okay, how hard it is to copywrite? You probably would like to know the six psychological sales triggers, wouldn't you, at this time?

The answer was yes, huh?

Okay, let's talk about copywriting a little bit.

Here's the little secret that no one is telling you.

All the latest high-tech Web design gadgets, bells, and whistles won't help you make any money unless you learn to use words and sales strategies that have been proven to get attention, generate interest and desire.

This is your pencil working here.

And motivate people to take buying action now!

Hurry up and write this down.

All the latest high-tech Web design gadgets, bells, and whistles won't help you make any money unless you learn to use words and sales strategies.

Just write that part.

That has been proven to- this is the important part-get attention...

Just write down get attention.

…generate interest and desire, motivate people to take buying action now.

And for those of you who are getting the recordings, you'll get to hear this time and time again.

It doesn't matter how pretty and professional-looking your ad, sales letter, or Web site is. The only way you're going to make money is by using words that communicate clearly the benefits of your offer.

Communicate clearly the benefits of your offer.

And the reasons why your prospects should buy from you rather than anyone else.

Remember talking about unique?

Communicate clearly the benefits of your offer and the reasons why your prospect should buy from you rather than anyone else.

These things are so much more important than how classy-looking and pro-looking your ads are, or your Web sites are.

Persuasive words and strategies that get your reader-I want you to write all this down-attracted to something that will be of benefit to them, then enough desire for that benefit must be generated to motivate them to take action and buy now.

I'll leave this one up here for awhile.

Persuasive words and strategies to get your reader attracted to do something that will be of benefit to them, then enough desire for that benefit must be generated to motivate them to take action and buy now.

Attracted to something that will be of benefit to them, then enough desire for that benefit must be generated to motivate them to take action and buy now.

Everybody got it? If not, get it from the person next to you.

Here's the big secret, folks.

It's the words that do selling.

You have to write your sales message so that your prospective customers develop an emotional desire for what you're offering them, before you ask them to buy.

This is the reason why long copy works.

You are building up emotional desire.

We all decide with emotions and then justify with logic.

You've heard that said. I'm going to give you all the reasons why this works.

Your ability to write persuasively is the most important and most widely overlooked marketing tool that you will ever acquire.

Everything else is bells and whistles.

Being able to communicate persuasively is the thing that makes things happen.

Three Basic Things That You Have To Line Up For You To Make A Sale

There are three basic things that you have to line up for you to make a sale.

Guess what they might be?

The right market, the right offer, the right time.

The right pond, the right bait. Come on!

And they've got to be hungry!

Very good.

The right market. They've got to be easy to find and reach.

This is all part of copywriting, by the way.

Because you can have the greatest sales letter in the world and if you throw it in the wrong pond, guess what's going to happen?

Zip.

They've got to be easy to find and reach.

If you can't communicate with them, how are they going to understand what you're selling?

Hungry and starving is preferable.

People who are already interested, people who are already motivated, people who were already buying and buying repeatedly. And if you have a list of these kind of people, you have a goldmine.

The right offer. Use the five Ps. We'll talk about that in a second.

The perceived value and the resulting benefits to the buyer have to be much higher than their cost. When you buy something, do you want to pay more than something is worth?

No. That would be foolish, wouldn't it?

Why would you expect anybody else would feel any different? If you are asking somebody to buy something from you, don't they want to feel like what they're buying is worth more than the money they're giving you?

The answer is, "Yes!"

Okay, does that make sense?

Folks, some of this stuff is like a whack in the head with a 2'x4', isn't it? It's like, "Okay, well that's how I feel about it," and then in the same breath we'll turn around and ask somebody else to do the exact opposite, because we're trying to sell something now.

That's what I mean. You've got to hop on their side of the table and see life through their eyes and their mindset.

The five Ps in the offer. There's a simple way to come up with offers.

The promise. Include the three biggest benefits.

Now this is kind of basic stuff, but if you can do this we've got you 80-90% of the way there.

The product. Give a detailed description of the product.

The package. Okay, we've got the product. Are there any other goodies to go along with it? Any bonuses?

The price. Is there any special pricing? If it's not a special deal, tell me about the price of competitors. Maybe you cost less. Maybe you cost more. What are the reasons why you're doing each?

The penalty. Is the time limited? Do we have quantity limits? Is the price only good at this for a certain period of time?

This plays into scarcity, which we're going to talk about in a little bit. Scarcity makes people jump, right?

Right time.

You've got to write this down because this is hard for people to understand.

People buy when they are ready, not when you want to sell them something.

In my younger years…oh, that's hard to say. In my younger years that was one of the hardest lessons is that people just did not care that I needed to sell them something. And the more I needed to sell them something, the less interested they were in buying. Until I finally figured out that people were only going to buy when they wanted to buy and not when I wanted to sell them something.

Now, if that's the case, if I'm having to wait until people are ready to buy, what does that tell you that I have got to do if I'm going to have sufficient cash flow?

I've got to be throwing my bait out in front of a lot of fish, right?

Continuously, and in volume, and in ponds that produce.

Do I really want to try to educate people and convince them to buy something?

No.

I want to spend my time finding ponds of fish that are gulping at the surface to bite on whatever hits that water. Right?

That's the marketer. That's different than sales.

Sales is convincing and persuading; marketing is finding people who want to buy it, and then letting them have it.

How I Got Nine Times The Sales From Ten Minutes Of Work

And persistent follow-up. Here's where people really drop the ball. They don't follow up, follow up, follow up. I've got some examples that I could show you to where on a three-step program, and I consistently have done these kinds of numbers and sometimes a lot more, where 90% of the sales came from the second and third follow-up.

Of the total sales that had happened in the campaign, if I stopped at just the first try, I would have only gotten 10% of the sales.

Now let me say it another way. By taking another 10 minutes that week and mailing again, I increased the profitability by 900%. Nine times. And it took me how many minutes to do that?

And it was basically; remember that thing I sent out two days ago, "Well, here's a reminder."

And remember that thing I sent out a couple of times this week? "Well, it expires tomorrow." That was the gist of it.

So follow up is pretty important. I've had other situations where I just did the follow up and it increased the sales result, instead of if I stopped at the first one, there is one example where out of the total, the first mail that went out produced 3% of the total sales. By doing the second and third follow-up, I increased it by 43 times, the profitability of the campaign, because I did the follow-up. If I didn't follow up I would have had 3% of the profits.

Does that make sense? I got 97% of the profits on the second and third follow-ups. That's how important it is to let people to know things two or three times.

The Psychology Of The Buying Process

Okay, the psychology of the buying process. There's three steps to it. You already know this; it's a repeat. Does everybody want to chime in?

Know you, like you, trust you.

We have the quick studies here. Good.

Okay, this is worth your trip again. The six psychological triggers to use in every ad, sales letter, or Web site. You need to put this on an index card and stick it next to your computer, and every time you write an e-mail to somebody, I don't care who it is, you need to work your way through these six triggers in this particular order as I will tell you in a moment.

Now this comes from a guy who wrote a book, I think it was in the 80s, by the name of Robert Cialdini. I usually talk about this every time I speak publicly, because it's had that much influence and it's been worth a lot of money to me knowing this stuff. He wrote a book called Influence: The Psychology of Persuasion.

How many of you have read it? How many have read it twice? Three times? Five times? Ten times? At least, okay?

Cialdini was a university professor, and thankfully he was the kind that got out into the real world and did something with himself. He took a sabbatical from, I think it was Arizona State University where he taught. He went out and got sales jobs, and he hung out with the top salespeople in a variety of industries. What he was trying to do is he was trying to figure out how salespeople get people to say yes, and buy.

He distilled it down into six basic areas, of which most people miss it that there is actually a seventh, and it's in the preface of the book.

He says that the greatest thing you can have on your side is really good product. That really does help.

Given that, here are the six things he discovered. Now, he doesn't have them in this order in his book. I've taken the six triggers that he discusses and reveals, and put them into an order that works better, I believe, in the sales process.

The first of which is, you need to let people know that either you or somebody you know that you're endorsing, is an authority expert.

Is anybody here an expert?

Yes! Those hands are going right up!

Good! All right, we established that today, right?

If people perceive you as an expert, they will respect your opinion and believe what you say is true and worthwhile. Now the reason these things work, you have to understand, is that how many of you are busy? Right . Everybody is busy.

How many of you just love, when you do a major purchase, to have to do all the research all yourself, and wade through everything and read volumes of information and technical manuals and specifications and all this kind of stuff just to make the purchase. It's time-consuming, it's hard work, you've got to think. Right?

How much easier would it be if you could pull up Consumer Reports and see that they did all the test driving, they did all the ratings, and they gave it four out of five stars. Doesn't that help speed up the process for you?

Okay.

These six psychological triggers is what happens and why it works, and authority expert is one of the reasons. Like Consumer Reports, are they positioned as an authority expert? Absolutely. That's their whole game, isn't it?

Can you do the same thing in your market? Absolutely. By reviewing stuff. Don't say everything is great.

Every rose has what? Thorns.

Every toad has warts.

Isn't it good that while you're praising things, to always mention something that's not quite right about it. That makes everything more believable, doesn't it?

Okay?

By the way, you might want to write that down and circle it.

The second one is liking. Remember know you, like you, trust you? People do business with people they like.

Think about purchases that you have made. Do you like to buy from people that you don't like? I go out of my way not to buy from people I don't like.

The third is commitment and consistent behavior. This is where baby steps comes in. You go for small commitments and you ask for other small commitments, and once people start saying yes, they fall into the habit of saying yes to you, as long as you don't ask them to do more than what they're comfortable in committing to during the process.

This also helps you build the trust part of the know you, like you, trust you. They take one step with you, and they don't get clobbered. Then they take another little step with you and they don't get clobbered. So what are they learning? They can take a step with you and they don't get clobbered. All right?

In other words, it's a good experience each little step of the way.

Now do you ever want to clobber them?

No!

You love these people. These are your customers. These are the reason that you're in the business, right?

There are other people that see, and I am not going to mention names, but there are other people that see customers as their enemy. It's a battle. I always thought that was a weird way to look at it.

Reciprocation. Do something nice for them first. Many times, not always, people tend to reciprocate and give back. Always remember that there are 360° in a circle, so don't be upset if people don't reciprocate directly back to you.

Social proof. If others think you're good, you must be, right? That's what social proof is all about; testimonials and endorsements.

Scarcity. People tend to want what is scarce. Great offers that truly have time limits and/or quantity limits, price reductions, whatever it is. When I say truly, you need to be telling the truth on all this stuff.

Now what Cialdini found out is that most salespeople will use one of these six things in helping to get people to say yes. And as I was reading this and learning this stuff years ago, I said, "My gosh, if this stuff works if you just use one of them, what if you packaged all six of these things in everything that you did? Wouldn't that be something? And each one builds on each other?"

Now, if you want to see an example of this, save my e-mails to you. Just start collecting them and analyzing them and see if you don't see this. Now some of this is really, really subtle, because I can do it in like two or three paragraphs. I mean in a sentence; I can put about three of these things in there and you don't see it. It's all underneath the radar, and I'm not going to give you examples today. You're going to have to read them.

But I'll bet you, if you go back to the page that described this weekend and if you look for all six of those things, I'll bet you will find it on that page.

Here's a hint; that I use them in every communication that I do. Now I do it on a, I am kind of programmed to do it now. You will learn to do it by wrestling with it and try to get all these things in an order.

Now I'll tell you the next thing I did after I learned all this stuff. I started going back through old, classic sales letters, like over the last hundred years to see if I could spot this. If you go back through Dale Carnegie, the "How to Win Friends and Influence People," those sales letters that sold millions of dollars of a $5 book; that's a lot of books over the years.

You'll start seeing this pattern in this order time and time again, to where I actually expanded this to where I have a report that I put out on it. It's called, "17 Parts of Every Successful Ad, Sales Letter, or Web Site.

If you go to this address, www.internet-success-system.com/saleslettertemplate you can get a copy of that report. It will walk you through the 17 steps of crafting your sales letter, and if you follow that you'll be able to write sales letters that work.

It's not that I dreamed that up; I just went through all these classic sales letters and saw a pattern. That's going to give you a track to run on.

Now you may find that a couple of spots down around 11, 12, 13, 14, right around in there, you might flip them around in order depending on how the flow is going. You're not going to be swapping like 12 and 14, you might swap 12 and 13. It's that kind of thing. It's really, really subtle.

But to begin with, just try to work your way through 17 things and see if you can't get it to flow pretty well. You're going to have to connect the pieces so they flow from one section to the another,

The Best Way To Learn Great Sales Copywriting

One of the greatest things that you can do, and you want to write this down, is you want to get hold of some sales letters that are really, really good ones. Stuff that you buy from would be a starting spot, right? Because it got you to buy. And you want to print those out on paper, get away from your computer, and get a yellow notepad and write those down in your own handwriting.

"Well, it seems like a lot of work, Mark."

Well, do you want to make a lot of money or not?

Now why does this work? Here is the reason why.

You hear me doing that a lot, right? Here is the reason why. I don't expect you to do anything without telling you why.

It's that when you get that out on paper and you've got your yellow notepad and you've got your pen in your hand, you're reading with your eyeballs off that page and you're memorizing maybe ten words at a time, depending on how good your memory is. As you do that you're probably mouthing those words, too.

So you're seeing them, your lips are moving, it's imprinted on your brain, just to get it in there long enough in your short-term memory so you can do what with it? Have it come down your arm out your fingertips onto the pen and the ink on the paper, and you start moving your hand.

Now what happens when you start moving your hand? You've got to remember what you just read, and now you are in the process of putting that down on paper. Physically involved now, right? And now you are also talking to yourself, right?

Think about this process. You are probably saying the words as you scribble them because you're having trouble remembering what it said when you read them. So now you're scribbling the stuff out, and what happens when it's your writing coming out on the paper?

What are your eyeballs doing now? You're watching it again, and who's writing is it in? Yours!

You begin to own these magic words that have sold millions and millions of dollars of products and services. It becomes ingrained in your brain. You're programming your brain to be a great, world-class copywriter, if you will only do this simple exercise like I tell you.

And you do the whole sales letter that way. Then once you get that one done, do you know what you do? You do another one, and another one and another one; and you fill up that whole notebook with great sales letters. You will start spotting patterns and phrases, sub-headlines, and titles, and headlines that work.

How To Create Offers Using The Five Ps

Offers. Remember the five Ps of the offer? You start seeing the sales strategies that pop up off of the page, and then as you read in your normal daily activity the different sales letters and ads, you will start seeing this stuff. You'll be able to analyze it logically. You'll see all the moving parts, and the interesting thing is all these things that I'm telling you about, you will be able to analyze them.

[Laughter]

Even though they're being shot out at you, they still work on you on the emotional level.

At the last ISS conference (www.internet-success-system.com), I was talking about our Gold Membership Program. I was telling people the benefits of it, and I was explaining the thing, that if they wanted to sign up for that they could, and this, that, and the other. As I was up standing and talking about it, one of the gals raised her hand and she says, "You're doing it to us right now, aren't you?"

Everybody looked at her and I said, "What are you talking about?"

"You are using those six psychological triggers right now."

I said, "Of course I am. I told you I was going to."

In the meanwhile people were… Right, Steve? People were coming up the aisle, signing up left and right, and they all knew, I revealed everything to them, but this is how strong this stuff is on the emotional brain.

But you've got to use it.

Okay?

So now you know.

Yes?

Participant: Everyone who goes to hear Harv Eker in his three-day, three weekend thing, always says that you cannot believe the stampede of people going up to pay $3,000 for this program, $10,000, whatever, because of this very thing you were speaking of.

Mark: Exactly.

Participant: One other thing. Bob wrote on a thank-you page, "Thank you for seizing this opportunity."

"Thank you for seizing…" and I said, "Take that word seizing off! It sounds like there's a knight in shining armor coming to seize your child, or…" I mean, it just didn't feel right to me. He said, "Myrna, listen. I read that so many times and I learned that the word 'seize' is important!"

But it just didn't feel right to me. It felt like too strong as a thank-you.

What's your thought on that?

Mark: The only thing you can do is test, because a lot times what we logically think or feel about something, you have no clue because you're not the market.

Participant: "Thank you for seizing the opportunity to purchase this $9 tape?"

[Laughter]

Mark: It's kind of strong to me.

There Are Certain Patterns Of Language That Generate Action

Mark: I'll tell you a story. Go ahead, I can save the story

Participant: One thing that some A-level marketers are using in their signatures at the bottom is the things that are like "carpe diem" or things of that nature, that subtly and subconsciously we recognize. We know what they mean and so we act on them.

Mark: Right. Yes, there are certain patterns of language that generate action.

Participant: I was also thinking as you were talking about the six triggers and how you can let people know that you're using the six triggers, but they still would respond on an emotional level is, my thought about it is, you have already tapped into their desire. So really the words that you are using are almost, the fact that they know that you are using words is almost a side issue because their desire, it has now been exposed.

I thought about it, like we know that we want to buy a car. I know that I want to buy a car. I need a car, I want a car, I'm going to buy a car. You go into a car place and immediately you've got a car salesman. Well, we all know what car salesman are. They're here to try to sell me a car and get the most money and make me feel like all these things that I don't want to feel, like I'm being swindled. They can do all they want, but the bottom line is you want a car, and they know that coming in.

So even though they're a salesperson, you know they're using all their tactics, the bottom line is your desire almost overrides that fact and you walk out with a car in the end. So it's sort of like that concept too, it sounds to me.

Mark: What's the most important thing to you as a seller?

Having a market that wants to buy.

[Laughter]

Didn't I tell you that this was easy? The hard part is getting on that side of the table to where you understand what it is that people want to buy, and don't argue with them.

Have you ever been in a sales situation where somebody, you knew you wanted to buy something and you were ready to buy right now. The sales page was just a formality and you were pressed for time, and you're ready to write the check, sign the paperwork and, "I'm out of here!"

Right? The salesperson said, "Oh, but wait!" It's like they wanted to get through their whole sales pitch.

[Laughter]

That's a dumb salesperson. Me, if somebody says, "I'm ready to buy now," I shut up.

Okay? Who wants to jinx that kind of sale?

Yes?

Participant: I have got a great story that will illustrate that and you can have it and you can use it whenever you want. I have got a colleague who is from another country, and he doesn't have a whole lot of driving experience. He decided he wanted to have a Mini Cooper, so he went to a Mini Cooper dealer and he brought a friend with him who was actually going to drive home the Mini Cooper that he was going to buy. Then he could go out in the parking lot and practice with it before he went out on the roads.

Well, the salesman, it wasn't enough that he wanted to buy the

Mini Cooper, he had to take him out. Well, he stalled the thing out driving out of the dealership, and before he got to the first corner he had already run it into a curb and created $3,000 worth of damage on the vehicle. Never had a release, never had a signed sales contract, anything. He ended up buying a different car from a different dealer. The guy had the sale as soon as he walked into the door, and not only did he kill the sale but he created $3,000 worth of damage, also.

Mark: [Laughter]

Oh, my goodness!

Participant: I wrecked my car in the rain one day and was really upset and the guy at the office said, "Go drive a Honda Prelude. I had never been in one, so I went to the dealership in the city and asked for a test drive. The guy let me go, and when I got back, he looked at me and said, "How was it?"

I said, "It was absolutely orgasmic."

[Laughter]

He looked at me and said, "I don't have time right now, I have to take delivery." He never asked me for my name or my phone number or anything. He looked at me and said, "I don't have time right now."

I am like, "I just had the ride of my life! Okay, I'll call somebody else," and I did. Two weeks later I drove up into the parking lot and asked for the sales manager. I spoke to him and said to him, "I was here two weeks ago and I took a ride in one of your cars."

He said, "Oh, yeah. The beautiful Prelude over there."

I said, "Yes, that's the one I drove, but you see this is the one I bought from another dealer, because this is what your salesman said to me when I came back off my test drive and told him it was an orgasmic ride."

I had so much fun doing that that day, because I couldn't believe a man would stand there and do that! I mean, he had a sale in his hand!

Mark: Right.

So by using these six triggers, we worked people through the three steps of what? Know you, like you, trust you. Great.

Expert authority, liking.

You've got these written down?

Commitment, consistency, reciprocation, social proof, and scarcity.

Okay. Now, the reason I walked you through that, remember the little page that Louis put together? You can see it here. There it is. He builds rapport with the people because he is one of them, and he talks about the problems that they have, and he gets on their side of the fence, and he asks them the question.

It's like a little, mini sales page, isn't it? He just kind of walks through and its really easy. Here are all the benefits; he's bringing out the benefits.

All they have to do is put in their name and address and click a button.

Now how hard is it to write something that long? It's easier than 30 pages, let me tell you.

What?

Well, he is not having to make the sale here. He's making a sale;

there's a transaction happening, make no mistake about it. Remember, here is the transaction. It's the e-mail address and first name in exchange for the e-book.

He is not having to do the dollar transaction. Now the dollar transaction is bigger, therefore you're having to spend more time, if somebody doesn't already know about the product, hasn't been endorsed to it by somebody that they know, like, and trust, then you have to build rapport, you have to get into their mindset, talk about their problems, how they're trying to solve them, talk about their goals and their dreams, introduce the product, point out the benefits of the product, make it unique in the mind to where you're positioned in the marketplace on the top end of the things, make the offer, talk about the price, talk about the guarantees, get them to click, get them to do that now!

Hey, it's a lot harder than this; just getting them to trade an e-mail address and the name, right?

His thing that he's trying to do here is build a list of people who are interested in golf, and at the same time, immediately upsell them on a product that he thinks they might be interested in. Now some of them will go for it now, some of them will go for it later, some may not go at all. But it sure is a good way to build a list, where you can maybe break even or make a profit instead of lose money.

Where You Should Put Your Subscription Signup Form

Participant: I have been told that on an opt-in page or a name squeeze page, which I guess is basically what this is, you should try to put the opt-in form above the fold. Obviously this one's not. How important you feel that is?

Mark: It all depends. If all you've got to say is this much, then put it above the fold.

Participant: So you are saying it is not really necessarily the most important thing. You want to make sure you convey the message first, before you can get to an opt-in page.

Mark: Let me show you another one. How many of you saw this this week?

Here are two pages: one, two. Two folds, whatever you want to call it. There's a very simple little headline, a little benefit, benefit bullets, and how do you get it, right? And you fill it in.

Remember what happens on the next page? The guy has the audacity to ask you for referrals even before you saw the thing, and you know what? People fill this in.

Here you download the thing, and here you can tell some friends.

Now this has been up there for quite a few years; I just happened to send it out again this week.

There's another one I did a couple of weeks ago, now that was at www.hunteridge.com/3words.htm - so if you are listening to this later, you know where it is.

There's another one, www.hunteridge.com/findsell.htm - "How to

Find People That Will Buy What You Want to Sell Them."

Both of these things are chapters out of a book that I offer for sale. I just took some of the chapters that I think would be good bait, then put them in a single e-book form, and that other one, that "Three Words" thing is only four, maybe five pages long.

That's a really good lesson for people to know.

Here's another one, "How to Find People That Will Buy Whatever You Want to Sell Them." Once again, the same format: here are all the benefit bullets.

I actually ask for referrals before they even get to sign up for this one. They don't have to because I let them off the hook here, and if they don't want to do it, they can jump down to the bottom of the page and "Click Here" and they're off to the next page where they can download it themselves, or they can sign up for themselves, rather.

It tells them how I am going to send one e-mail out and I tell them that I am only going to send one, I am never going to use it again for another purpose, and guess what? That's the truth. I have never, ever accumulated those e-mail addresses and mailed to all those people.

Now there have been thousands and thousands and thousands that have come off of this page.

Participant: [Inaudible]

Mark: I don't think it's available anymore. There's another one called TellAFriendPro that's really good, and I think it is a www.tafpro.com I have got a copy of it and use it on another site and I like that one. You can run contests and all kinds of stuff with that one; it's fancier than this, though. It costs more, too.

So there are two simple ones, and these are not anything that are beautiful but people sign up to get the free e-book, and they recommend other people to come to it also.

Okay?

So there are a couple of examples.

How To Quickly Get Something Going To Make Money

- Audio Four Transcript -

Mark: Okay, let's start with a new question.

"Starting with no money, I have time, interest, desire, determination, no retirement fund, age 65. What's the best way to build a site which will earn $5,000 a month? It must increase within 3-6 months on the Internet; I'll be using this as sole income.

Okay, how to quickly get something going, we already talked about that. The quickest way to get something going is find out what people want to buy, and you sell it to them.

[Laughter]

That's the easy process. The other thing is like the model that I showed you there that Louis did. By the way, he gave me permission to show that to other people as a model. It's to build your list while you are selling things. You can drive traffic to that site in how many different ways?

Let's see. You've got a newsletter. Just jot these down as fast as you can, okay? Newsletter and just abbreviate.

Search engines, pay per click, articles, PRWeb, news groups, forums--other people's and your own, affiliate programs, joint ventures, cross-promotions, giveaway promos, exit traffic, teleseminars, viral e-books, viral software, podcasts-audio or visual, trade ads with some people, do endorsements, contests, thank-you page cross promotions, grant reprint rights to others, give testimonials, and your loyal un-subscribers, which is one of my favorites, which generate thousands of dollars a month to me.

I make money off the people who don't even like me anymore. Undisclosed. Thousands. Tens of thousands.

Those are people who don't want to hear from me anymore, who unsubscribed and when they unsubscribe they get sent to a page that makes them other offers, to other people other than me, because they don't like me. So I refer them to other people and they buy from them and I get paid.

Don't you like that one? And on a lot of stuff I get paid repeatedly and that's where it ends up being thousands and thousands of dollars a month.

By the way, write this down.

Do the work once to get paid forever.

And you can even make money off of people that don't like you; those are your loyal un-subscribers. That came from one of our Internet Success System mastermind conferences. We were sitting around having dinner one night and we dreamed that one up. I told guys what I did and somebody said, "Yeah, it's your loyal un-subscribers."

So that's been a standing running joke.

Okay, once again all those.

Newsletter. That's how you get traffic to your site. Search engines, pay per clicks, articles, PRWeb.com, news groups, forums, your own forums, affiliate programs, joint ventures, cross-promotions, giveaway promos, exit traffic, teleseminars, viral e-books, viral software, podcasts--audio or visual, trade ads or endorsements with people, contests, thank-you page cross-promotions, grant them reprint rights, give testimonials, and your loyal un-subscribers.

Now last weekend, Steve, it took us what? Three hours to get through all that? Because I went step-by-step through all those things and all the ins and outs of those.

(Note: Mark is referring to www.GrandmasterOfListbuilding.com)

What's The Best Way To Earn Money With Resale Rights Products?

Mark: "What's the best way to earn money with resale rights products?"

The thing you have to do, if you're going to do resale rights, thousands are buying the same rights as you, therefore how are you going to be unique?

You're going to have to somehow package them up and do something different. You are probably going to have to change the sales letter a little bit, you are going to have to change maybe the bonuses that you offer, you may even need to put a new book cover together. Okay?

The $100 that you spend on doing that will make all the difference in the success of your campaign. Like Louis is really good at this. He buys resale rights to all kinds of stuff; he knows his market, like the golf thing. He looks for little niche markets like that and he will put together in just a little bit of time an attractive cover. I mean it's not stellar, but I mean like the golf thing. I can't do that; I thought it was great.

He goes over to like www.iStockPhoto.com - I think it's $1 per picture, so it's not a whole lot of money. You get complete rights to use it, and there's a bunch of those kind of sites out there; stock photo sites. You want non-royalty.

So you've got to make your resale rights offers unique.

"Is it still possible to become an Internet millionaire?"

Yes!

"And consistently earn millions of dollars every year?"

Yes!

"is there a best niche to do it in?"

Any one that's got enough people who are willing to buy what you have found to sell them. That's going to be the bottom line. If your niche is so small or people are not used to buying on the Internet, it's real hard for you to make money on the Internet. So you want to make sure that the market that you are involved in is used to pulling out credit cards and buying on the Internet.

Does that make sense?

Is There A Best Way To Build A Site?

Mark: "Is there a best way to build a site?"

No.

The best way to build a site is where the site has focus and we have talked about it before. In our own mind the focus is a one-mindedness, where everything else goes away. Guess what you need to have when people visit your site? You want the rest of their world to go away.

Anything that distracts them from your communicated sales message you need to get rid off of your site. If you've got little flashy things around the edges, what's that going to do to your main sales message? It's very distracting. It becomes like a flea market. You've got all kinds of stuff going on and you're looking this way and that way, right?

So you absolutely want to have the pages have focus, have them set up to where there is one thing for that person to do. And your content is what kind of content? Actionable. You're trying to lead them to the next step, whatever that next step is you want them to take. That's really, really important.

Participant: Mark, what about the sites that are just brochure sites? They're completely a waste isn't it? Like wearing Donna Karan but not doing anything about it.

Mark: Yes. If you're not asking somebody to take action, you're just a brochure. I mean, most brochures in the brick and mortar world are worthless. They just tell you about the company. Nobody care about your company; they only care about themselves and what they want to solve or the places they want to go. If you can help them solve problems or reach goals then there's a reason to talk, otherwise you're a waste of time.

The Best Advice To A Newcomer To Internet Marketing

Mark: "How would you advise a newcomer to Internet marketing?"

The best advice is to understand the marketplace. You keep hearing me say it over and over again, and I hope it sinks in. You've really got to understand the emotions of the marketplace. Not on the superficial level but way down deep. What really eats them? Because that's where people will start taking action.

In this thing that I wrote years and years ago, I talked about the three brains that we have. I don't know if you all have ever read what I wrote about that. But physically you have three brains. You have a brain stem; the reptilian brain, it's called. You have what's called a mammalian brain, which wraps itself around that brain stem. Then you have this gray matter, which is our logical brain, the human brain. Okay? Our thinking brain.

Of course, humans are really proud of what? Our logical brain. We are the thinkers, right? Yeah, right.

The mammalian brain is the herd mentality. Mammalians: love and family, herds, togetherness, we feel safe, and all that kind of stuff.

The reptilian brain is the thing that when you take your finger and put it on a hot stove, how long do you have to think about this before that hand comes off of there? It's an immediate response happening on like a low level. Okay? It's built into you.

Now, which one of those brains would you like to be talking to, if you are talking about having somebody buy what you are selling? The logical brain, where they like to think about it?

No.

You want to be talking to that low brain, where there's a response mechanism built in. Where I want it, I desire it, I've got to have it!

Now let me work you through those three brains. Have you ever made a presentation to somebody, whether it be sales or you are just trying to communicate your opinion on something, and the person says, "Well, I've got to…" What?

"Think about it. I have to think about it."

Now what does that mean? They're not going to think about it. They don't have enough information to think about it. They're not going to take the time to research it. That was just, "No." But they're going to think about it, okay? That's the top level brain.

"I'm going to logically analyze the problem." Ha!

The next level down, have you ever heard anybody say, "You know, I need to do that"? That's the next layer down, and what happens when people say, "I need to do that"? They don't do that.

What happens when somebody is really under the gun and they hear about something and they go, "I've got to do that."

Now this is the need to, want to, got to, kind of a situation. I need to do it; I am going to think about it.

I want to do it, now we are getting closer.

But I've gotta do it, now somebody is motivated. You want to get people to the gotta stage, or you want to find people of who are in the gotta stage.

Five o'clock in the afternoon, April 15th, and you haven't done your taxes and you need help. How willing are you to pay somebody at that point and time if you think you are going to owe money and it's going to cost you at least 10% more if you file the next day. If you could find one that would help you, you'd pay him, wouldn't you?

Yeah.

So a lot of it depends on the timing and various issues; how much up against the wall you are. How much motivation that you have at that point in time when somebody makes a presentation to you.

That's the need, the want, the gotta.

"I have no list, nothing set up. What is the easiest and the fastest way to getting started making money?"

We kind of talked about that. The fastest, easiest way is to do that article trick, the 12 articles, stick it in a PDF book, get something that looks like something of value, that actually has good actionable content that leads them to something else, put up a Web page that gets their name and address so you can build a list, you deliver the stuff to them and then you stay in touch with them once a week. Then you send them bits and pieces of that special report over time.

"Mark, I gave it to him in a PDF book, now you are telling me to send it out to him in an e-mail?"

Yes. Do you know why? Because they won't read the PDF book. They will get it and look at it and say, "Boy, look at that table of contents. That looks great! That's a nice looking PDF, that's something of value, I've got to read that." Then the phone rings, right? They're off to doing something.

How many of you have done this?

I know you have, right?

They always tell me, "Oh, no. PDFs are valued more highly and people will spend the time and read them." Sorry, look at your own behavior. You only have to look in the mirror to be entertained, right?

I mean, I do it, too!

[Laughter]

Do you all ever go to the mall and just watch people? Yeah? Do you ever do that? We have a saying around my house. "I only hope that we are also as entertaining to others as they are to us." Because it's got to work both ways, right? Because for every person sitting there and watching somebody else, there's somebody else sitting right there watching you, right?

Isn't it true?

How To Turn A Free PDF Ebook Into A Six Figure Income

Participant: Mark, I would like to ask you a follow-up question to that. Last weekend when you were talking about Louis's product that he had put together over just a few hours which you put up a little while ago. If I caught it correctly, you had said that if he wanted to, which he may or may not want to, that he could probably parlay that into like six figure income. Based upon what you said already, could you kind of flesh it out and give a little bit more of the detail on that linkage or that line of events would be if a person wanted to actually take something like that and use that as the vehicle?

Mark: Sure. Everybody can help me do this and this would be a fun project in the next five minutes. We're going to show how to make what you just saw there that he did, building a list to golfers by starting out with an e-book, 12 articles he got from somebody else. Then he found one product that he immediately could use as an upsell to the free offer.

What else could we possibly do?

Now remember, these are golfers. Is there anybody here who plays golf? Okay. You're nuts, right?

Okay. Self-admitted, completely insane regarding golf, right? It's the most interesting, fascinating, and frustrating game ever devised, right? Where one shot can be the most beautiful thing; it's like a work of art. And the next shot is like whoosh! Where did that come from? And the harder you try the worse you do, and the more you get yourself out of the way, the better you shoot.

What fun is that? It doesn't make any sense to me, but we still go out and do it anyway.

So what else would golfers buy if they actually felt that Louis was one of them, and he is. Okay? Because he will tell them all his duffer stories, too, and he will talk the way golfers talk, and he will talk about the trips he took so they'll know he's been places. Maybe he gets hold of some special, super-duper putter that he tries out, and he gets three of them that he tries out. Now he has got a line in some custom golf shop, and he took this golf tour package down on some island.

Do you see where I am going with this? This is all the stuff that golfers want to do, and he just works them through step-by-step. What else can help me?

Okay. What else would golfers buy? Trips, vacations, golf cruises! Now think about that. Golf cruises. Do you know what golfers do on cruise ships? They knock golf balls out into the ocean, because they've got to practice the swing, because once they get to land, where do they go? The golf courses, right? So they work on the swing by knocking balls into the ocean. So they never go into the woods that way.

[Laughter]

That's right!

What else? Various clubs. I mean, Big Bertha and her sister, too. Whatever her name is. I mean all that stuff.

Now, is that a competitive marketplace? Absolutely. He who has the rapport with the market, wins.

Rapport.

Okay?

Know you, like you, trust you. Believe me, Louis is a real affable fellow; I mean really likable. You like him, and he has learned from me that you put your personality into it, and you let your personality show. You don't try to hide.

What else? Golf lessons, golf videos, golf tapes, mental golf tricks. How to calm your mind on the golf course to where you and the ball are one, this kind of stuff, right?

That's right, all kinds of widgets that make you swing better and do the motions better, and that kind of stuff.

Clothing.

How about match-making? Find the girl of your dreams who loves golfing, too. I don't know, we're making this up as we go, but can you see that that's going to add up from a couple of bucks to $10 to $100 to $1,000 to $10,000 to $100,000. We have a $100,000 business. Congratulations!

Participant: Staying healthy

Mark: Where's that coming from? Uh huh.

Participant: Staying healthy. I can send them my e-books.

Mark: That's right you can cross over to the e-books on staying healthy.

Participant: One of the things that you might be able to do is if you know of a golf portal that has an affiliate program, a referral program. If you don't want to actually be doing all that legwork to arrange for all those tests of those putters or those cruises or all that, if you've established a rapport with your customer base and you know of a portal that you could refer them to, then you might be able to go pretty deep as far as commissions or sales through that portal.

Mark: I'll suggest something to you, that the more you can relate to them about a specific product and direct them specifically to that page, the higher the likelihood that you will make that sale. If you send somebody to the front page, what happens? There's all this stuff, and people get confused and lost. You just sent them to the flea market.

But if you can send them, if the affiliate program at a portal site like that is set up correctly, you'd be able to send them through an affiliate link to a specific Web page. Then get it to happen that way.

Now just think if you found a few of those businesses. Multiply that times $100,000.

A lot of the stuff you see is duplicatable, and once you know how to do it in one niche, you just move to the left or the right into the next niche and you start another one.

You may have to do a few of them before you find one that hits like that, but you just keep doing it and doing it and doing it.

How many of you play around with AdSense? Some people make a ton of money using AdSense on their sites. Do you know how many sites they have? A thousand plus. That's how that game is played. You're making $10 a month, $10 a day, whatever the number is, from a site. Now if all you have is a one Web site and you are making $10 a day, what do you get? Three hundred bucks a month, right? You can buy a used car for $300 a month, but that's not exciting, is it?

So instead of one site, we've got to have a hundred sites, and now it gets more exciting. Or a thousand sites. So it's a matter of numbers. The problem with that business model is it's run by Google, and when Google decides to change how their search engine works, all of a sudden the traffic you've got can dry up, unless you have done one amazingly simple thing, which would be what? You'd built your own list. If that's the case, you used Google and you got the benefit out of the game.

That's the thing that people are missing so much when they play that AdSense game, is they miss building the list. They have all that traffic flow, and they're good at getting the traffic through their sites, but they forgot to build the list of people who they can contact time and time again.

Because most of those people would never come back another day, and all you are doing when you build those kinds of AdSense sites, you are just selling eyeballs to somebody who is really selling something.

You are selling advertising space. Nothing wrong with that; just know that you are missing a huge opportunity by not building a list and staying in touch with those people.

MARK HENDRICKS

How To Leverage Up The Typical AdSense Type Site

Participant: If you have an AdSense site, and you don't have a capture page, how would you incorporate that into your average AdSense page?

Mark: I would just put an offer there instead of the article. The AdSense sites typically have articles or some kind of content, whether it is some kind of RSS feed that's really a directory built some place else, or wherever. Just do a page like that. Some people won't go for it; other people will click the AdSense stuff.

Oh, by the way, do you want to know another way to monetize this game, like this golf game? In the newsletters that you send out like once a week, which are those articles that are a repeat of everything in that PDF book that everybody is going to recognize, but they won't; because they didn't read it. Guess what? Even if they read it, they won't remember it. How many of you people remember what you read last week?

I'm a realist. I report; you decide. Who says that on TV? One of those news things, right?

It's what I see happening, myself too. I can't remember all the stuff that I read last week. I go through it so fast; the stuff that's really important sticks with me. The rest of it is someplace down here, low-level. It all stays there, you know that. It's all there; it's just how good is your filing cabinet?

So what can we do? Instead of giving them the article in an e-mail, couldn't we direct them to a Web page? In that e-mail that gets them to a Web page, there's that actionable article. It's going to lead them to something.

What else could we have sprinkled around the edge or right in the reading path? Yeah. AdSense ads.

By the way, MSN about three weeks ago, just opened the gate. You can go to adCenter.MSN.com - and set up your ads there. Not AdSense, but you can buy ads like Google AdWords; you can buy ads and have it populated on MSN search pages.

Why is that interesting? What Web site automatically opens up when somebody gets a new computer and they have Internet Explorer? MSN. Do you know how many people in the world have no clue how to change that? Anybody in this room? Shhh!

Not in this room, this is the hip crowd, I know. The Google crowd is Internet savvy; they know how to change the startup page to something else. That's how tech-savvy we are, right?

The other majority always open up the day fresh to MSN, and your ads could be there. So if you have got, like a mass-marketplace kind of thing, where it's not real tech-geeky kind of stuff, you might be better off using MSN. MSN ads at adCenter.MSN.com

Then the other one, the big player, is Yahoo. It's called SearchMarketing.Yahoo.com. That used to be Overture. SearchMarketing.Yahoo.com

Now Yahoo does have a publisher's network now, and it's kind of getting off the ground real slow.

What To Do If You Have Limited Computer Skills

Mark: "I have limited computer skills so what's the least expensive way to get a Web site up and running?"

I am going to tell you, that the first thing you need to do, if you're trying to do business on the Internet, you're going to have to get really good on your computer. You're going to have to know real tough stuff like copy and paste, cut and paste, but here is the big one. You are actually going to have to know how to find files on your computer, and where they are stored, and creating folders.

[Laughter]

Now we are getting some giggles out of this, but I am dead serious, folks. This is one of the biggest stumbling blocks I see when people say, "I really want to do this Internet marketing thing," and then they download like a piece of software that I sell, and they can't find it on their computer.

I see people's elbows going into people they know here.

You need to get like that video professor guy that's on TV all the time, whatever his name is. Buy his thing on how to do XP, or go to the local bookstore and get one of these bright yellow books for dummies. Right?

AOL is for dummies, believe me. No offense. I don't want to talk about AOL now, that's okay. AOL is a fine company.

[Laughter]

But that's what you need to do, and get one of those books at the bookstore, whatever the topic is, and just work your way through it page by page by page, and learn that computer. How to find files?

Here are the tools that you are going to need. A computer that you can get around on; and if you are Mac user, I have got news for you. Go find yourself a used PC. Is anybody a Mac user? I sell software and it's never going to be written for Mac. Sorry.

Participant: Yeah, but Mac will run XP on it.

Mark: Yeah, most of the time it's compatible if you have one of those gizmo programs, but so many times, I mean Mac users love their Macs and I understand all that. This is an emotional thing. Yep. See? Yep!

Okay, but if you want to be part of the other world, of which 95% plus I guess is PC-based or something, Windows-based, the best way to do it is to go buy yourself last year's model of computer; a used one. Upgrade it to XP, which is easy to do, probably it has already got XP on it, right? Maybe for $300. It's getting cheaper and cheaper and cheaper to do this. I keep hearing, "Yeah, but you really have to do it for Mac," so I'm not going to waste my words on that again, right?

But you've got to be able to find your way around the computer, because the next step is when you ftp, when you have a Web site, you're going to have to move files from your computer up to your Web site. If you can't find them on your computer, how are you going to upload onto your Web site? And your Web site is up there in never-never land.

It's like you can't touch it, so that's the other piece of the puzzle. Now that we know our way around the computer, how are we going to make Web pages? Well, you are going to need some kind of a Web page editor, I would suggest that you do not spend any time at all learning how to do HTML code.

I'd suggest that you get something like FrontPage from Microsoft, DreamWeaver from Macromedia or da-da-da-da-da-da...

www.123WysiWyg.com from moi. Me. And learn those systems to where you can, basically do, "What You See Is What You Get." That's what I mean by WysiWyg editor. The price range goes from $97 for 123WysiWyg up to $300 or $400 or $500 for the other ones.

Learn to use those systems and just design simple Web pages. If you haven't built a Web page before, let me send you to a page where you can watch me do one in 22 minutes; and not only one page but a whole little Web site in 22 minutes.

Go to www.123WysiWyg.com and WysiWyg is "What You See Is What You Get," the acronym. 123WysiWyg.com, and about two thirds of the way down that page, once you get to the page is a video where you can watch me build a Web page of about six or seven pages, or something like that. It's complete with links and graphics and all that kind of stuff, in about 22 minutes.

The thing to do, no matter what HTML editor you are using, is watch that video like two times through so that you get the gist of the whole thing, then go back to the beginning. Every time I do one thing, put it on pause and do exactly what I just did, and then once you did that, then you take it off pause and watch the next one thing and hit pause again.

If you will do that, in about three evenings you will be able to make Web pages that will make you money, and you will be able to link, and put graphics in your pages, and link to pages, and link off your pages, and all kinds of stuff. But you are going to have to spend a few nights and actually do it.

Yes?

Participant: Mark, on Butterfly Marketing, I purchased this out of complete emotion and the box is still there. This is like six months ago, and I haven't touched it. Is WysiWyg easier?

Mark: It's a whole different thing.

Participant: Can you explain?

Mark: Yeah, 123WysiWyg helps you build Web pages. Butterfly Marketing is an approach to basically one-time offers of upsells. In other words, you get somebody in for a freebie or a low cost thing, and then you upsell the next thing. And it's software designed to help you do that.

HTML Sites Vs Just Using WordPress

Participant: What do you think of the trend towards using blogging software instead of designing Web pages, and just running whole operation like that?

Mark: Okay. Like we talked about this morning, the great thing about blogs is they run off of RSS technology, which search engines like because they can either refer people to content, or pull content off of blogs by the way of the RSS subscription button. So that's why it is so popular.

It's pretty easy to use. If you use WordPress, well, like with Blogger.com, you can set up an account, and be blogging and typing in there and creating pages within minutes. Google owns it, so do you think Google is going to scan it and index it? Yeah. It's their territory; it's their turf.

WordPress. I had blogger accounts and I used it for awhile and it had some links back to my sites. I wasn't doing anything naughty or anything like that, but it got blocked out of Blogger.com. So I wrote to them, and of course they don't bother answering. They won't explain stuff, so fortunately I had been in the process of converting the whole thing to WordPress. I had most of it already converted over, so that was a great time for me just to go to WordPress.

So if you go to www.hunteridge.com/blog you will see a WordPress blog of mine and back issues of all these e-mails that go back for ever.

Now what do I do for the content on a blog? Guess what? All the e-mails that go out that get response get stuck up on the blog for all time. So when people find the blog, they've got a few years of reading to go through. These things are the money pits. In other words, these are things that made money for me, with all the links to all the products, and all the six psychological triggers built into them, and all the offers for other little freebie goodies that build my list, and everything like that.

So these are like the "best of" up at the blog. If you are publishing a newsletter that you send out like once a week, that's like your test thing. You are always testing the market and always coming up with something new. "Here is the new stuff that I found, here is what I'm talking about, here is what is going on." Sometimes people will respond to the stuff. Sometimes they don't. This stuff that they respond to, copy that and stick it up on the blog.

Do the work once and get paid forever.

If it's an article that happened to catch the interest, I did a thing a couple of weeks ago. The thing was called "Work Smart." Does anyone remember seeing that? That was an acronym for a bunch of other things that I talked about in a conference that I was speaking at.

So I put that in an e-mail and I get all these people asking me if they can reprint this on their pages. So what do you think I did with it? Well, I guess this one I should maybe stick up on my blogs, since I'm getting people asking me to do the same, right? And should I submit it to other article directories? Yep. And that's the one that within a week or two, I see it like in 500 places. All I did was to submit it to my article directory site and those ten other ones. I didn't mess around with the other thousand.

The thing that I go for, is give me the thing that will do 80%, maybe 90%, because the other 10% is too much work. I've got too much other stuff to do. Have you ever felt that way? I mean, let me go for 80-90% effectiveness, because the other 10-20% is going to eat up too much resources, and I'm better off taking that time and using another technique that I can get 80% out of.

Now other people will focus and focus, and they will get like 99% out of this thing, but they also go nuts trying to go for the extra 1%, and they miss all this other leverage.

Watch Out For These Mistakes, They Can Happen Easily

Participant: Mark, when we were in Florida two meetings back, there were a lot of the speakers who referred to disasters that had happened in their careers; losing their entire list, and things. We talked a lot about affiliate marketing and JVs and everything. Are there some things that we should primarily build our structure with to prevent disasters and getting ripped off. Or are there common things that happen?

Mark: Yeah, I mean, people steal from you, sure. I mean, I find every once in awhile that somebody will, well this 12 Days of Christmas thing. It was either the first or second year, I can't remember which. The guy, whoever it was, they just took my whole page, stuck their name at the top of it, and did their thing.

There's a real easy way to deal with that. First, I write a nice letter to them, saying, "Excuse me, there seems to be a problem here, a copyright infringement." invariably, as a third grade child would, they write back saying, "I don't know what you're talking about."

So I write back one more time and tell him, "You've got 24 hours to get that off of there, because this is what's going to happen. I will contact your ISP and they will shut you down for copyright infringement."

They will write back invariably, saying, "I don't know what you're talking about. I haven't done anything."

Twenty-four hours pass, so now we're into 48 hours. I get all the ISPs, give them my Web site, give them their Web site, and point out that on my Web site it says copyright whatever year, and I consider it copyright infringement. I am not after you guys, I am after the person who is infringing, but it is hosted on your server.

So who's got the deep pockets here? The hosting company. It usually takes about 10 minutes before I get a call back, and they want to talk first. They want to talk to me and see what's going on. I say, "Thank you," and I'm very polite and pleasant. I haven't threatened anybody along any path. I'm just stating facts, and saying here is the next step, here is the next step.

At any time you want to co-operate with me, I am a nice guy, I will drop the issue. I am not going to press it further as long as I get my way, because I am right! And you have stolen from me.

So every time I have gone through this; it has been maybe three or four times over the years, it usually takes maybe a third day. Then what has always happened is the ISP shuts down their domain, because the person would always say, "I didn't do anything wrong, and I came up with that idea." The ISP, the hosting, they're smart people to begin with, they're business people. They see what's going on, they're not willing to risk their business for some shmuck who's trying to rip me off.

So their domain disappears. Now who's mad at who? That's when they start talking to me. Now I get the letters back saying, "You dirty rat, you made us lose our hosting account."

I did. Now it's my fault that they did something of criminal nature, is what it was. I was nice enough to say, "Look, are you going to co-operate? Take it down and I go away. You go your way and I go my way," but invariably I had to go through those steps, so yeah. That happens.

Now at the break I mentioned that, somebody asked me, "I see all these sales letters, they all look the same, and don't people get mad at you stealing it?"

Now the question may come from these what you call, resale rights packages, you know they provide these sales letters? If that's the case, all those people absolutely do have the right to use that sales letter. Now how effective is it if you see the same sales letter about the same product?

Think through this resale right stuff, folks. If thousands of people are going to buy this, what's the value of this thing? In about three weeks, you can't even give it away on eBay, much less sell it on eBay. It devalues very, very quickly.

So be careful when you get caught up in these resale rights packages. If you know how to repackage, re-bundle, and make them unique looking, then go for it. Or if it happens to be a product that you personally would be interested in and you could use, like a piece of software or something, go for it.

Many times, I am not going to say most, many times the software in those resale rights packages still need work, unfortunately.

Now back to the sales page. If you do see some somebody ripping off a sales page or with the same sales page, think first that it might be resale rights situation. Otherwise it may be somebody is stealing somebody's sales letter, and that's pretty serious. I mean, that would really bother me.

But the other thing that happens, and I encourage people to do this, emulation is good, modeling is good, theft is very, very bad. So I don't mind people who model.

There is one fellow, my www.Market-Soft.com site, I found somebody who had put a different header, all same words were there, the whole thing.

It was the same situation. I wrote to them and it was the same scenario. "I didn't do anything." I said, "Look, Pal."

[Laughter]

I actually went to the ISP level, and then I think that they got hold of that guy and the guy wrote back, and he says, "I apologize. You're right." He says, "Mr. Hendricks, I have re-written it and I would like you to take a look at it, and if it's okay with you, then we will go with that."

I went back to look at it, and he did. He rewrote the thing. I mean, I could still see the influence, but it wasn't word-for-word. All the psychology was still there, and the flow was all the same. I didn't mind that. Just don't steal it word-for-word, sentence-for-sentence. Re-write, emulate, model, that's fine. We have all done that.

Just don't steal. That's not good.

Participant: On this topic of copyright infringement, I know that there actually is a process that you're supposed to go through to copyright your work. It's not just putting those @ words there, though I think that's what most people do. They don't actually record it in some kind of...

Mark: Actually the law is, if you look it up, the act of putting it out to the public is copyright.

Participant: So there is no form you need to fill out and kind of make it formal.

Mark: No form is necessary. Okay? The next step is putting the little ©, copyright, the year to kind of put a date on things, who claims the copyright, which is you or your company. The thing about filing with the copyright office is if there is an argument about it later, then there is a piece of paperwork in the copyright office, with a specific month, date, time and year and your name. It's registered to give it some kind of date and that it's registered in your name, and you did that. So if it came that far, then you'd have a piece of paper that would help in your case. Not make your case but help your case.

But once again, if you have a problem, find out who has the most to lose if you were to pursue it. Remember how I said like the companies who provide the autoresponder service and you're their customer? If ever it comes to choosing between you the customer and the big ISPs, who they're trying to get deliverability, and you get accused of spamming, the chainsaw comes out, and your limb gets cut like that. No questions. You might be lucky to get your database back from them.

By the way, if you're using third-party service like that, make sure you keep a copy of your database, because at any point in time something like that could happen. Or what happens to computers once in awhile? They lose data, right?

Now they backup and stuff like that, but you should keep your backups of that, because that's your business. That's one of the nightmares if you lose that, because then you'd be starting from scratch again, building your list.

Protecting Your PDF Ebooks

Participant: I have got two questions, please. Would you comment, please, on using PDF files which can sometimes be copied-you can set them up so they can't be copied; versus using eBookPro?

Mark: Yep. eBookPro is a PC executable file, right? The problem, and there are other ones with the same problem, since XP came out with the SP2 upgrade to the XP, a lot of EXE books, you know the kind of PC e-books? If you download those things, and if some of the pages inside try to access Web sites, you get one of these warning pages saying, "Cannot Connect." That's because the SP2 security function of XP is blocking you from accessing the Web from your computer through an executable file. That's because a bunch of virus and scammers, and all those kind of people, they would create PC executable files, that would do all this dastardly stuff around the Web and do the Phantom Menace to your computer.

So that's why PC e-books have gone the way of the dinosaurs, somewhat. I have a little gizmo that I call PCeBookFixer , that people can get. It toggles back and forth between setting your security patch on XP and being able to read these PC e-books. So that's the difference.

The other reason why you want to PDF e-books is so that MACer's can use them.

Participant: Um hmm. Right. Well I know eBookPro, you have to register the book and you can only use it on your computer, and you've got all those security codes, and that's just too damn much trouble. I mean, I'm not that paranoid.

For a long time I used ReferenceUSA, which is a database from the library. What I used to do was copy the page off so that I could paste it into Word so that I could always have it there for reference, and one day I just couldn't copy. Well, I thought that was something wrong with the computer, and I tried for weeks to do this. I called the library; he couldn't answer the question. Finally I called the number at the bottom of the page and said, "What's the gig here?" They said, "Oh, you've probably noticed that our software people set it up so that you cannot copy the page."

I was wondering if other people, now this is a database. You can download parts of the database but you can't copy it anymore, unless you copy the whole page and then your Word coughs and chokes and dies. Are people going to get into a mode where they're going to make sure you can't copy what's on their page; you can't copy and paste?

Mark: Well, you can set up stuff now, there are scripts that do that. Now there are ways around it. Anytime, if there's a programmer who can make it do this, there is another programmer who can make it do the other thing.

But how do you slow down the other 99% of the population that's not a programmer?

Participant: Okay. I have noticed that I have hit some pages I couldn't copy.

Mark: Right. There's pages that you can't see the code. If you go try to look at the source code and there's nothing there.

Participant: You can just do print screen.

Participant: Oh, I know that.

Mark: Okay, but you want to copy and paste the words. Who wants to type?

Participant: Yeah, but your scan program will convert it to words,

OCRs

Mark: What else?

Software I Use To Create Info Products

Participant: Before you go to that sheet, I would like to interject a question. You've been talking all along about how you can create products from various and sundry methods, and also you mentioned that at the start of this event that you will be creating an info product from today's session and tomorrow's. So with that in mind, I wondered if you could kind of explain the software that you are using to do that, and how that works and some of the features, and how we might be able to model that.

Mark: Okay, let's talk about teleseminars. Here's an easy way to position yourself as an expert, remember? And it's also an easy way to create a product, because you don't have to leave your house, your guest doesn't have to leave the house, and all of your attendees can be sitting at their houses, too, or office, or wherever they're at in the world; driving around with the cell phone on their heads.

There are two different teleconferencing groups that you might try. The both work in a similar fashion.

www.freeconferencecall.com

www.freeconferencecalling.com

You can be on there, I think it's for 6 hours at a time. You don't have to make a reservation, they have a really cool piece of software once you figure out how to get to it. You log into your account and there is a thing which you click and it will open up a new window, and you can actually see who is on the call and all the phone numbers. If you catch them where people like introduce themselves when they come on the call, you see a new phone number come in. If you click on the phone number and they announced their name, you can type in their first and the last name, and the next time they call in, it remembers that. So you can always see all the people on your calls. You can set up conferences anytime you want to. So both of these are terrific things.

Now why do these companies do this? They also sell services like 800 numbers and toll-free conferencing, where people call in on the toll-free numbers, guess who gets to pay that? The host. But with these free ones, everybody dials and pays their own long distance.

It's free. They use it as a lead generator.

Participant: There's a little problem that I wanted to ask you about. Three times in a row I was on a call and we heard another party.

Mark: Like cross-talk between another party?

Participant: Yeah. What happens when it keeps happening like that?

Mark: You just move on.

Participant: Use another number.

Mark: Well, I mean, you have to continue your conference; it's not like you are going to sign off 150 people and say, "Call back."

Participant: But what if you are recording and there's this interference that continues?

Mark: Well, you would either stop, or you would edit that stuff out. Or you try to speak up, and you take a moment and say, "Excuse me, the person who has the three barking dogs in the background, would you mind hanging up? Because there's about 250 people here, listening to you yell at your family." So usually, if you just take a moment to do that, then the person will leave if that's the problem.

Somehow they've gotten in there and the wires are crossed somehow, and then yeah, that's going to be on your recording, but guess what? It's really easy to edit that out, once you get a copy of it.

Participant: Do you have the software that will edit?

Mark: Yeah, we'll talk about that.

So you can record them and make products for lead generation or sales.

Here is the basic equipment, okay? Dictation Buddy is the thing that you see me using right now. It looks like that and it's $34.95. From that, you can edit and cut and paste and put things together, and you can slow it down. If you're trying to find a spot; see, all you have to do when you edit, you have to find a silence to start the cut, and you have to find another silence after the bad section. You find the next silence and you mark those two spots, and you do a little snippy scissors thing and that's gone. Then the two points on the outside of it go together, and all of a sudden this cross-talk thing is gone and nobody knows about it.

Or if you get to talking about a subject that you don't want to have in the product, just do a little snippy-snip and that's gone. So you can edit these things after the fact.

The nice thing about this is that you can find these spots and you can fast forward it, like speed it up like one-and-a-half times; two times. You go through it and it sounds like chipmunks talking, and you get through it real quick. Or if you're having trouble finding the silent spot, you can slow down the speed so that it's real slow, so that you are able to click that edit spot in the silence.

So this is a pretty quick and easy version, and you get that at HighCriteria.com. Go to over to their Web site, HighCriteria.com, and look for Dictation Buddy. They've got a bunch of different other software that is a little fancier, I wouldn't go that direction. If you just want to go this way first, I do the Dictation Buddy. It's pretty neat.

Now you are going to need to go from your telephone. Now the things that you're going to need to make good recordings from your telephone is not a wireless telephone. I am not talking about cell phones either. Cell phones don't work well and wireless telephones like everybody has in their houses now, they don't work well either. You want to have a phone with the curly-cue wire to it, to where it is a landline kind of thing. One of those old-style phones if you can still find one, right? Go down to Goodwill and see if you can find yourself an old phone; the old-fashioned kind that works.

And one where the dial tone is not in the earpiece, the handle thing. You want the dial tone on the foot pad of the phone. Okay?

So we go over to this Web site, which is at OmnicronElectronics.com and we are looking for the thing called the TSA-3PC. If you look around their Web site you will find that, and here is a picture of how it works. If you are listening to this later, just remember that you need to go to OmnicronElectronics.com. The homepage, look for TSA-3PC.

That's a telephone handset audio tap, and the way you work this thing is there's a little box which you attach next to your phone. It plugs into where you would normally plug the handset into the phone base. Do you see this little gizmo here? That wire goes in there; there's a wire that runs from this new box down to the input of your audio sound card for recording purposes. Then you take your telephone with the curly line and you plug it into the other spot on this little box. That's how the electronics work. It also has a little screw set that you can adjust the volume.

Now what that does is, when you pick up the handset, everything goes on in your ear or coming out of your mouth is going to get recorded into your computer.

Create whatever file you want to make; WAV, MP3. That's what the Dictation Buddy does. It will record it to PCM or WAV or MP3, or whatever it is.

Also recommended: Audacity and Sony SoundForge

 Yes?

Participant: If I have a mic and I'm recording into my computer, it's very clear, but when I record it on the phone it sounds very hissy; the "S" sounds. Is this better, or is it just the phone?

Mark: How are you recording it?

Participant: Audio Acrobat.

Mark: No, no, I mean where is your microphone plugged into to do this?

Participant: When I record something to use as audio on my PC, it comes out very clear. When I record a conference call, it comes out not great.

Mark: Right. How are you getting the sound from the conference call to your computer?

Participant: Audio Acrobat.

Mark: That's the software. What wire or microphone are you getting it to the computer with?

Participant: My phone. I record it on the phone.

Mark: How is the phone connected to your computer?

Participant: The phone is not connected to my computer.

Mark: Audio Acrobat is a software in your computer, but you've got to get the signal from your phone line to your computer somehow. How is that happening?

Participant: There's a third party somehow.

Mark: I don't know. Here is how to do it.

 [Laughter]

Now by nature, telephone is always going to sound tinny, because the frequency response is not as great as a regular microphone.

So that's why, let's continue and I'm going to show you the upgrade here in a second. You can get headsets from Radio Shack, the kind that connects to a computer sound card. The one that has the microphone on it that's designed to go into the sound card, that's where you're recording directly to the soundcard. That's not what you want for telephone stuff.

The other one that we want is the kind that has a microphone designed specifically for telephone stuff. That's the thing which is going to be connected into the TSA-3PC telephone, so you're going to have a headset where you get to talk, where you don't have to mess with a handset and have to hold this thing all the time, which is really clumsy.

So this thing plugs into the little box, which is a TSA-3PC, and acts as your telephone, and you may also need this thing called the Radio Shack headset/handset switch, product ID 43-2017, or something comparable if they have upgraded that. That allows you to switch between the headset one-way switch; the other way switch goes to the handset, if you want to talk on the handset.

Now the problem inherent when you record telephone

conversations, is you being the host, will be louder than your guest. It's just the way telephone technology is. So, better quality. Now we're going to step up to the real world of some pro line kind of gear. This is a super pro line gear, I mean you can spend $1,000-$2,000 to get this.

Like the radio stations, do you ever notice that when somebody calls in and the volume level of the guest is the same volume level as the host? That's what we are trying to fix here, and you can spend $750-$1,000 to get one of those kinds of gizmos that will do that; and that's just for one gizmo to even out the volume.

For the microphone, I like the Audio-Technica AT3035. That runs about $200, but it's a terrific mic and you can use that for audio interviews or for your recording stuff directly to your PC. You can use that to really get a good sound where you don't sound tinny at all.

That also requires a power source called a Phantom Power, and there is one that is reasonable for maybe $20-$30; the Rolls Mini-Mic Preamp, the MP13. You can pick up both of those at a Web site called www.MusiciansFriend.com

If you don't know your way around like the high-tech music business, there's an 800 number on that site. You call them up and just tell them, "I want to order an Audio-Technica AT3035 and also the power source Rolls Mini-Mic Preamp MP13," and they can package that up and have it to you overnight, if you wish.

** You can also get the AT3035 as a USB Mic now, that's the way to go!

Now the little magic box that is going to even out the voice levels, you and your guest, is a thing produced by JK Audio and it's called That-2. It's a little black box and it has a few different inputs, and a button to either go from the headset mic or the fancy mic. You can check that out at JKAudio.com/that-2.htm. That runs, it seems to me, maybe a couple of hundred bucks.

Now as far as recording software and editing software, a real good home studio program is Sony's Sound Forge, and you can pick that up at SonyMediaSoftware.com. That has all kinds of really cool graphic editing capabilities where you can see where your silences are, and the wave forms and everything like that. It really makes editing a lot easier in real tight spots, because you can blow the thing up to where you can see all the squiggly lines and really get in there tight, and edit. It's like word-processing on sound, is what it is.

Okay?

Did that help out?

Then the way you get to use them, or learn them, is just practice with them before you have a teleseminar. Get some friend of yours on the line and say, "Hey, I've got this new software, and I need to kind of figure it out, and would you mind just talking with me on the phone for awhile?"

So you practice your levels and you see how to set levels and stuff like that. On digital recording, you never want to get into the red. Red means it's clipping, it's distorting. As long as it is green and into the yellow just a little bit, you are okay. If you ever see red, you have gone too far.

Let's talk about video for a second. Camtasia runs about $300 and it allows you to, whatever is on your screen, on your computer, it's going to record that and any audio that's at the sound card, it's going to record that at the same time. That's about it. There are editing capabilities, where you pull in, here is one from last weekend that I pulled in and pasted in there. Can you can see the squiggles building there? And here it's playing, believe it or not.

I am not doing anything, that's it playing. That's me talking from last week, so I get that and then I can edit this. I can stretch things out where I can see that audio track more, and if I want to edit I can highlight that, and if I hit the scissors, it would cut that whole section there and paste it back together again. So I don't want to do that. I'm going to get out of that altogether.

So Camtasia is pretty neat like that. The other editing software that you might want to look at for videos, is Sony's Vegas Movie Studio. I would go for about the $129 package, it has a few more bells and whistles than the $89 package that I think is worth the extra $30 or whatever it is, $40.

Do you all know what a green screen is? Have you heard of that? Do you know how the weather, when you watch the weather, and a person is standing in front of the screen and they look like they're pointing at something on the screen? There is nothing behind them; it's a green screen. It's green cloth or green paint on the wall, and they're actually looking at a monitor off-stage. They're just standing there, making these motions and talking about how it is 88° in Baltimore today, and it's partly cloudy, and stuff like that.

Well, you can get these green screens; you can get one at Chroma-Key.com. They sell this cool little thing in a special combo. I have one of these, and it's a stand and this Chroma screen, that if I had a video camera here and I had the Chroma screen behind me, and I was taking pictures, it would show up green. But I could insert different backgrounds. I can make it look like we're doing this from some Tahitian island resort; and change backgrounds and all kinds of stuff.

Have you ever seen these silly cartoons of people flying around and there is stuff going behind them? Well, they're recorded it with this green screen, see like this girl here. If you are listening to this recording, if you are at Chroma-Key.com, there is a gal on the left side in front of a green screen.

So what will happen is when you do the video editing, like with Sony Vegas Studio, you can put a different background behind her. So you could be doing a video show and have a real cool background that looked like heavy duty news-at-eleven background, and that kind of stuff. You could have things moving behind you and all that kind of stuff, or any kind of background shot that you want you slide in there. So that whole package there is $239. It's 11'x12', so it's sizeable, okay?

All right. So that's kind of multimedia, like a real quick view of how to do some of that stuff, or at least the software that you would be interested in. If you have any inkling toward technology, audio has been here for a quite a few years. Video is the next thing, and you see all the big companies beefing up video right now, because it's going to be like watching TV. It's going to be like cable TV on the Internet. That's where it's all heading.

Participant: With that in mind, Mark, you mentioned Camtasia, which that just records your screen, your computer screen. But I think the video that you are referring to that we're about to move into more, is a camcorder, some kind of camera taping you. Can you touch on that a little bit, about any tips you have about how to get up to speed and something on that.

Mark: Yeah, the thing you want to look for in a camcorder is to make sure that it is digital, where it runs off of a FireWire, which is kind of like a fancy USB if you're not up on what FireWire is. But most camcorders will have a FireWire, it's like an IEEE and some number. What's that? 1394, thank you.

It's also known as FireWire, and if you don't have a FireWire card in your computer you need to add that. Or for a laptop you can buy one of these plug-in cards, a FireWire card, so you can get the information in there.

Now that will let you go direct from the lens of that digital camcorder, and record onto your hard drive. So you're not having to go to a digital tape; it's direct recording to disk. Direct-to-disk recording. The other thing you want to watch for is to make sure that you can use an external mic and plug it into that camcorder, so that you're not using the cheapo mic that's built into the camcorder. You want to have a mic input on the camcorder to where you can take a microphone that is built for that kind of purpose, like even a lapel mic that's got a cord that you can plug in to that thing.

So you could have the camcorder in front of your face here, and within a couple of feet you could plug that microphone into it, and the sound that you're saying goes in the camcorder, through that FireWire. The video and the audio get to your Sony Vega. Vega is set up to where it is recording the audio and video at the same time.

If you have a cheaper camera like me, who didn't know this when I bought the camera, you will have to do it a little bit different. There is a gizmo that I have which allows me to hook into the computer input rather than the microphone input on the recorder. That way I could FireWire the video into the computer and I can go in the audio card on the computer and have it show up in my video recording suite. I can do it that way.

But like I said, the thing you want to do is make sure that, and for something like this you are probably looking at spending maybe like, the prices keep coming down. I would say it's in the ballpark of about $400 for a good, digital handheld recorder. You'll want to get a little tripod so you can put the thing on a tripod, so it's not shaking around. That will go to make things look a lot more professional.

Lighting is a big deal.

Here's how to do lighting on the cheap, where you can go to get these workshop lights. Instead of spending hundreds and who knows how much money on lighting, have you ever seen these cone-shaped things that are just metal cans basically with a light bulb? You can get those things with the clippie things on, that you would use like in a workshop? You can set one of those up kind of this way, and one kind of this way, and one kind of above you out of the shot, to give you that little glow behind you, right? It lights up the screen and evens the light out. Light is really important to video, because if you don't do that right, you get all kinds of shadows and it looks goofy.

If you use a regular light bulb, you look orange. So if you are going to use regular light bulbs, you have to get a blue film that you can get like at a photography store, and you just lay it over the front of those cans with the light bulbs. All of a sudden you get filtered light that the camera likes and you look correct again. Your complexion is the right color.

The other way to do it is, they've got these new light bulbs, I can't remember the brand name. It's like natural light or something like that. It filters out the orange light, so that helps along those lines. So if you ever see somebody doing video and they look orange, that's what is going on. They need a blue filter to help filter that orange-ish light out.

Okay?

Yes?

Participant: Coming out of the camcorder, what are you using? AVI? And what are you taking it to, FLV when you're making it Web ready?

Mark: Yes. Right, it's either going to go to SWF, which is shockwave kind of, whatever you call that stuff, or FLV, which is the newer format. The way that's converted, Camtasia converts it automatically for you.

Participant: Can you do full motion with that? Full motion video?

Mark: You know, I don't remember. I kind of learn on an as-needed basis because otherwise I get overwhelmed with the technology.

[Laughter]

Participant: Thanks, Mark.

Mark: Those are good questions.

They have ways to convert that, and there are free converters that will do that for you. The other thing they're really hot on is all these sites that will host this stuff for you, so you don't have any bandwidth problems with video. A year or two ago they were spending thousands of bucks a month just to host video, Internet video, because the bandwidth is so huge and expensive.

Well, now they've got it converting down to smaller file sizes, plus bandwidth is less charges. Now you have got places like Yahoo and YouTube that want video hosted on their site. Now what's the trade off? You're posting your videos up there and providing content to them, but that doesn't mean they're not going to change the game sometime.

So always have some backup plan.

With those things you don't have to worry about the conversion, you just send the files up and they will do all the conversion for you.

Participant: But that's a real good way to drive traffic to a site, though.

Mark: It sure is. It's really hot, because people are looking for videos and they see where that link is, and it goes back to your site.

Participant: Mark, is this product similar or comparable; I think there's another one that's out from Jim Edwards.

Mark: Jim Edwards, I don't really know their product, they both came out about the same time. I will only speak about this since I don't know about the other product. This really shows you how to use it as a sales tool, okay? The psychology of infomercials, how to script one, how to get talent if you're not going to do it yourself, the technology, the techniques, the editing, the whole thing. Whereas, like I said, I can't speak to the other one. Jim and Mike; Mike's a really good tech guy; the audio guy, the video guy.

But this one, since I had something to do with it, I mean they have some scriptwriter built into it. It's all kinds of CDs; they interviewed a lot of people who have got a lot of experience in this kind of stuff. The gal who does all the media stuff for Tony Robbins. And you pick up a lot of insight into what it really takes to make video work with this kind of package.

They're coming out with a new product, if it's not out already. This goes for, I don't know how much they're charging for it. We were selling it for $997 for awhile. They sold out of all the tool kits I guess that they had made. They've got another thing coming out, I think it's for maybe $97, that shows you what software to get and the basics. That kind of stuff. That's the kind of an intro to their whole thing, to where you can get going, and once you want to learn more about this stuff, you can get into the larger packaging and get the full insight into how to produce videos.

Mike Koenigs has been doing, he lives out in California, both these guys do, him and Rocket. Mike's been doing some pretty fancy video production for infomercials for a quite a few years, and he makes a good buck doing that. He's being nice to new people who want to see what it's all about, but he does some really neat stuff. He's really good at it.

Any other questions on this stuff?

Participant: Yeah, I really appreciate the information on the green screen particularly. I was wondering, I have seem to have remembered seeing, somewhere in the past, there was a similar type of thing for still photography. Have you heard of anything like that, where you can change the background without having to do the lasso trick?

Mark: They also make a blue screen, but if you're doing business stuff, the typical color would be a blue blazer or something like that. So if you have a similar background as foreground, then you don't get sharp edges, and you kind of blend into the background. That's why most of the time we are using a green screen, because not too many people other than leprechauns wear bright green suits.

Participant: I can answer your question about that still photography green screen and digital editing for photographs. If you have a green screen background it makes it a lot easier to cut you out of that picture, but you need really good software like Photoshop. He's right; it's called anti-aliasing. You can grab that color, it will grab all that color and you can control how much of it bleeds into the background and how much it doesn't. I'll tell you the truth, black or white works better for me than green or blue. You can get a halo glow in the hair, you can see through hair. There's your answer; good software.

Photoshop, yeah. There is a special tool in the tool palette, a couple down, a magic lasso grabbing tool, it just grabs all of that color. Or it has an eraser feature which erases all the background color, and it works really well. It's a bulky package to learn, but it would take me minutes to do it for you.

Mark, What's Your Typical Day Like? What Are Your Thoughts And Actions From The Time You Wake Up In The Morning?

Mark: Let me talk about one more thing, and then we will take a 10 minute break and that will bring us to five o'clock. Then I think we will be able to work through the rest of this page of questions. These have been good questions, so whoever came up with them, thanks. It's been good to get the conversation going this weekend.

This question is, "What's your typical day like? What are your thoughts and actions from the time you wake up in the morning?"

Mark: I get up early. I am an early riser. The clearest time is when my eyes are open, which some people aren't that way, I understand. I immediately will go in and the computer typically runs 24/7 unless I am shutting it down and trying to clear things out with like the DSL modem and all this kind of stuff. I will do that at least once a week.

I turn it on and check e-mail while I am checking a few other things, like sales reports and stuff like that, so it's thinking over this way and I'm doing some work over this way.

I take care of customers first, always. That's one thing that people have made mention of me, of how quickly I do respond to customer situations, and that's really important. And especially when I check e-mail and they've just sent it, and I immediately turn back around and give them the answer. That just blows their mind, and I mean, more often than not, I'll get an e-mail just a minute or two later that says, "I can't believe I've got an answer that quick back from you," and I'm thinking, "Well, why not? I'm sitting here and it's somebody I care about, a customer had a problem and if it's something that I know answer to right now, how hard it is to bang out the answer to it, hit the button and boom! It's done."

I don't know about you, but if it doesn't get done then, or if it doesn't get done in that hour, and certainly if it doesn't get done that day, what's the chance that it's going to get done? Because what's tomorrow like? It's a whole new cycle, right?

So I like to get things done and out of the way, and move on to the next thing. I do not like to procrastinate. I like to make decisions based on the information I have; if I'm not comfortable with it I will research it more and make a decision. Let me get as much information as I can. I am not real analytical; I mean, I am, but you would be surprised at how much I go with the gut.

I don't know, it's not so much as like sensibility. That's what I call it. You do your research, and I really trust my subconscious mind more than my intellect. Now I'm not stupid, but I do think pretty well, but I know, and it's everything that you heard me say today, I know that there is a brain inside this skull that's better than the one that I think with. I trust that one because it works on all cylinders, all the time. The top level one gets really tired and it wants to stop thinking. I have to fight to keep thinking and processing, but the other one is continually going. It never gets tired and it will always work on whatever I feed it, and it will pop up the answers any time I need them.

I have learned to trust that, so I don't mind making decisions once I get a certain feel about, "Okay, I have researched this, I see how it fits together, and for some reason, I want to go this way. "

I don't worry about too much of what's the reason, but I also know that, "Okay, I'm going with it, now I am going to let the other brain takeover and say, 'Okay, let's test,' and we do want to compare what we think is going to happen and what happens, and if what we think is going to happen doesn't match up with what happens, now we have some new information that I didn't have before."

Right?

Now that gets plugged in, and then the subconscious mind gets to work with this new information that maybe wasn't even available, right? And maybe the quickest way for me to acquire that information was to do the test.

Now I am not going to do something that really going to jeopardize everything without either thinking through things or testing it small first. But you can learn a lot from itty-bitty little tests that tell you a lot, so that you can build and build and build on it. That's how decisions get made.

Now for the rest of my day, I am usually up before the rest of my family. I get a lot of work done by six o'clock. If I didn't want to, I would probably be done in those two hours and go do anything I want to.

That's pretty much it, okay?

I could be done at six in the morning, however, work is a game to me so now it's time to have fun. So now it's time to like have a cup of coffee with my wife, talk a little bit, take Jon to school, come back, go for walks, play with the dog, or whatever. Then I sit down with the computer and work on some new projects, because I always have new projects going.

So software development, I am really into that now because that's fun to me. Once I found a couple of programmers who can keep up, and they enjoyed it, they like the challenge of working with somebody who is always pushing them a little bit more, a little bit more, and who really appreciates them too, because I tell them all the time. If they're doing good work I let them know that I really appreciate them. I send them bonuses that they don't expect. A hundred dollar bonus overseas, that's a windfall. So they appreciate it, so they like the relationship, too.

I get up early, I go to bed early. A lot of times a nap in the afternoon, I love. It re-charges my batteries. I get up and I'm ready to go again, and I usually am in bed by 10 o'clock, something like that. But it's really a lot of fun and I enjoy talking with people on the phone. ISS members call me up, either a scheduled consultation or coming out of the blue, "Hey, I'm having this kind of trouble, what do you think, Mark?"

JV partners, we always have got things going on, and coming up with new campaigns for this, that, or the other.

So you see, there is a certain spot; you've got stuff that you have to do every day, just to keep things clicking, and then you have projects that are coming up, and that you are thinking about; the creative time about those new ideas.

I am always doing little bit of research to see what's on the front edge. I am always looking for new products that people that like to hear from me, my list of readers, would maybe want to hear about.

And that's kind of it. Try to have a little fun and stuff along the way.

Then come to Baltimore and try crazy ideas. I mean, this is like a test to see if this kind of thing works. It feels pretty good so far, and I am having a good time, and I hope you are, too.

Okay, good.

Okay, let's take ten.

How To Find Affiliate Products To Sell Using Clickbank

- Audio Five Transcript -

Mark: Okay, Jeff wrote, how to generate an e-mail list, how to generate sales using ClickBank, and the best ways to make money on the Internet.

So we are going to try to do all three here at one scoop, using a piece of software called ClickBank Account Manager. Now you can do the same kind of stuff that this does, in a time-consuming and clumsy fashion over at ClickBank. So if you've got more time than bucks, then go that direction and if you have got bucks and can install it up your server, or for an extra $25, we will do it, the installation-in most cases it doesn't take very long to do it, then you can have a tool like this.

 Now once you get everything set up and logged in, you can update your data from ClickBank. So the product database, I update it usually once a week. It's been a couple of weeks since I've updated, so let's update it now. There's a little green thing down here at the bottom of the screen, it's going to update. It's going to take a couple of minutes.

Now what this is doing, and I will talk while it's doing it for us, it's going over to ClickBank and downloading all the product information that's in the ClickBank marketplace and putting it over to my server. That way I have got the data that ClickBank has over there, but I am able to manipulate the data. In other words, sort and find better, the way that we designed the search engine in this system, than what you can do over at ClickBank.

Does that make sense? You can find all that stuff over on ClickBank, it just takes more time and it's clumsy, right?

The other thing, this other button up here, it will go in and get all of my sales records of all the sales that I have made per month for the last 12 months, and keep information in the database even if it is prior to 12 months. So on a rolling 12 months, it always makes sure that it's got the last 12 months plus any other data that it has gathered prior to that.

So I can search on things like product searches and I'll show you that in a second, to where I can search through the whole database for the best products that are happening, up-and-comers that are happening, like we were talking about the other day.

I can find purchases; I can find out who the best affiliates are, so if I want to contact them I know who they are; payout reports, when did I get paid what, what kind of returns?

So product search; here is where we find things and we can search the database by keyword search, by the vendor name, product rank and its category, if it's higher than whatever number, gravity, which is a term that ClickBank uses to let you know kind of the sales momentum, if that means anything to you. Like if out of the whole product line up for sale there, how well it's doing compared to all the other ones in a time period. It's kind of weighted towards current to last few weeks, that kind of thing. Probably about the last month. They don't really tell you what it means, except approximately what I just told you.

Affiliate earned percentage and what was the payout, affiliate earned dollar is how much you make per sale and the percentage of sales that are referred by affiliates, and that's always interesting. Because if you see a high number of sales done by affiliates, chances are that it's doing well for them and it might do well for you if the target market is right for you.

Here are all the different categories and subcategories.

The easiest thing to do is just say, "Go find us all that stuff," so we click that button and I am not making a video cam of this, or a screen cam. We are just going to talk through it, so if you hear this later on.

Let me introduce somebody to you. Remember I mentioned a guy this morning who was done very, very well over the last couple of years; his name is Leo Quinn.

I know Leo has been in town, he's got to make it off to the airport here in just a little while probably, so here we even have stuff that's zero for sale, so they're not even selling it as an affiliate program; they're just using it as an order system.

Up we go to the top of heap here and we say, "What are the best-selling products in all of ClickBank?" and let's checkout gravity. This is going to be the one. Now each column you can click on and it sorts it.

Participant: Where do you buy this?

Mark: You can go to CBAccountManager. You can see the top-selling product right now is one by vendor DataProz, with a "Z: on the end.

This, if you click the link with the left mouse button, the sales page will open up. If you right click and do a copy shortcut and open up a new browser window, or you can copy and paste like in a redirect file. See, I did a right click and saved that. There's my affiliate link already made for me.

We'll just click here, it will open up a new window and go to the sales page for that product. So this is all about who wants to make $1,000 a day by just entering simple data from home. Apparently there are enough people that would like to, that they will buy this, whatever it is, $50 to learn how to be a data entry processor and work from home. How to take surveys and make money taking surveys. There is some interesting stuff here.

So there are all these different products that you can search for.

Now let's go back to product search and let's say that we want to limit it to some other topic, like "fun and entertainment." We'll do a search there, and it comes back a lot quicker this time, right? So the top-selling product in fun and entertainment is shared movies; people swapping movies on the Internet. iPods and these are all the topics, music downloads. All kinds of things here.

Now let's go back and let's say that we want to stick with fun and entertainment, but as an affiliate we want to earn at least $30 a sale. If you're going to take the effort, you might as well be paid, right?

Now that limits it to approximately 17 products in fun and entertainment, and now we can look through and see if any of these things will match our target market. How about "Play a piano like a pro online," and there is the guy. He is going to teach you how to play piano online and he is selling that for how much? $67, and you see the affiliate down there? That would be me, because that was my affiliate link we were using.

So that's the process of finding products.

Now you can also go through the database. Let's go business-to-business and let's see what we get, and find something which might apply to your marketplace. Hey, look at that! www.Market-Soft.com I wonder who owns that?

We may be able to find some things that the gravity is lower and are not as well-known.

Page rank maximizer. I would read through the sales page and if it is a halfway decent sales page I may get interested in it. If it has something that I think the people who depend on me for information might want to know about, if I'm really interested I might try selling a few. I might contact the fellow and say, "I just put a few hundred dollars in your pocket, would you mind sending me a copy?"

Or most of the time what I do if I am really interested and if I think there's a fit, I will go ahead and buy a copy, because I like to review it. I like to be able to say I own it and I bought it. I think that it comes from a different place in your heart when you are endorsing something that you actually own.

Does that make sense?

So if you are at all in a position to own the thing that you are endorsing, do that. Now what will happen many times is if you get back to the person and you've helped them create hundreds or thousands or ten thousand dollars worth of sales in a short time, the odds are that you might get your money refunded back is pretty high; they will gift you that. And that's fine.

How To Use Listbuilding And Affliate Marketing Together

Okay, so that's the kind of tour of that. Now how do you tie that into building a list? Well, it's kind of like what I showed Louis doing with that golf thing. You get your report of the12 articles, then you build a PDF file and you have the freebie, and that what you're looking for is a quick referral over to a sales page that you think is a likely target sale for the target market.

While you are building the list, whether it be from free traffic that you generate; did we go through all these things that will generate traffic?

Yeah, I did, didn't I? Yeah, some of you weren't in here.

So whether it be pay per click or free traffic or forums, or all these different ways you can generate traffic, you will drive traffic to that page and then have them sign up to your list, and immediately get bumped over to whatever the sales page is that you're trying to sell. A small percentage of people will buy, because this is the first time they've had anything to do with you and all of a sudden you are making referrals.

But that's okay, because if something is selling for $67, and let's say two or three or four or five percent buy, and you've got a bunch of people coming through there, you can easily pay for your pay per click campaign, right? And maybe turn a profit. If you even broke even, you would be doing terrific, right? Because now you have a list of people interested in that topic. You can contact them time and time again, not only about just one product, but many products. That's where the gold mine is, it's in the follow-up and the contact and the relationships; it's never the first product.

Participant: Do you need different domain names for all these affiliate sites that are being set up, or can you work off of several domain names, or do you need hundreds?

Are you following me?

No?

Mark: Well, it's late in the day. Do you mean, I just use them off of my www.Hunteridge.com site.

Participant: That's what I mean. You're just building more pages off your Hunteridge.com site, rather than having to have a different domain name for ABC affiliate program or XYZ affiliate program.

Mark: Yeah..

Participant: Well, I have read something recently were people are setting up mini-sites, and they're setting up like bunches and bunches of mini-sites. Is that different?

Mark: It's whatever purpose you need it to do.

Participant: So those are like ten mini-sites built on his site, on one domain name, right?

Mark: Right. I mean, we could have set up one specifically for the topic at hand, and it would look and smell and feel like that is completely about golfers and that's the most thorough way to do it.

Is it required to make money?

No.

If you find that it works without having its own domain name, then congratulations! It works. Test, test, test.

Clickbank Affiliate Software If You Have Your Own Products To Sell

Mark: Do I see a hand or a microphone someplace?

Okay, Lou?

Participant: Yeah, I just wanted to ask one thing about ClickBank. I know that if you have a dedicated domain name for a single product that you are going to show up in this kind of list. But if you have a ClickBank ID, Lou123, and you are using that to sell multiple products off of one site, your products won't show up in this, do they? The individual products?

Mark: No, just the one. Inside your ClickBank account there will be a spot in there, to where people are directed when it's product number one. To get multiple products and have them go into different pages, you have to use something like Adrian Ling's Easy ClickMate.

I think you can get there by going to www.Hunteridge.com/easyclick.htm

Yep, there it is.

It's like an affiliate software that drives ClickBank products; that's what it's designed to do. It's been around for quite a few years and it works really well, and that allows you to have up to 50 ClickBank products in one account. That's pretty handy for maybe $50, whatever he sells it for, $67 now. It installs on your server.

Did that help out, Jeff?

So basically you find products that are going to match your target, you set up a special report or freebie, you're trying to develop a list and sell products at the same time, and then if they don't buy they get reintroduced to it again. If they see it a second or third time, not a problem. Repetition works.

That's the quick way.

There's another e-book I recommend people read, it's called AdWords Magic. I can't remember the name of it but if you go to www.Hunteridge.com/awm.htm you can get to it. It talks about this whole scenario of setting up this particular style of marketing, and something I have been teaching to people for like 4 years.

I am too busy to write a book about the whole thing, and I alluded to it in e-mails over the last year or two. I told people exactly step-by-step-by-step, how to do it. This guy either dreamed it up on his own or he saw it someplace and did it, but he's actually put together an e-book that really explains it really well. So I just refer people over to that.

So do you see what I mean? I didn't have the time to make a product but somebody else did, and it is exactly what it ought to be. ,How easy is that for me just to refer people over to it, and I don't have to do all the hard work.

In the last couple of weeks, referring that just a couple of times, it's a few thousand bucks for a few minutes of work. But until you build the list up and build a rapport, it's hard to do.

How Many People Should Be On Your List Before You Start Publishing A Newsletter

Mark: By the way, how many people should be on your list before you start publishing your newsletter?

That's an interesting question.

One. Right.

You don't even have to find somebody else. Go get yourself a free Yahoo account to make sure that your system is working, and mail it to that one.

[Laughter]

You can use a pseudo name if you want to, on the Yahoo end of it, so you feel like you are writing to somebody else.

You just do it and you do it every week, even if it's just you that you are writing to.

I'm going to sit myself right down to write a letter.

Because what can you do with these things? You are going to do this once a week, though you can do it more often if you want to. I mean it's just you. You're not going to unsubscribe, are you?

You're going to report yourself as spammer?

[Laughter]

I mean, you can try that to see what it feels like, right? Send yourself a nasty gram back. You could have a whole little thing going on in your head here.

But you get used to doing it, you get used to doing the research and publishing it, you get a chance to develop a writing style just by doing it, but what do you get to do with these things? The ones that are good.

Because some are going to be good, some are going to be okay and some are going to be lousy, right?

Yeah, you have got your content. You're doing it, man! You are writing books, you are writing blog stuff, stuff that works. Where does it go? The blog!

Do the work once, get paid forever.

Okay?

Use the stuff that you do over and over again in different format.

Use Broadcast Emails And Sequential Followup Emails Too

Participant: Question. When you are building your list and marketing to your newsletter subscribers, are you building autoresponder messages into the future, or do you every time you send it out it's fresh right out of your brain, hit send.

Mark: Okay, we'll talk about that a little bit. Anytime somebody subscribes to something of mine, they get subscribed to three different lists.

Like if you went to that "Three Words" report this last week, you actually got subscribed to three lists. One was specifically to that report on the three words that's guaranteed to make a sales letter fail, and fix those and everything will skyrocket, right?

You also got added to a master list, and you also got added to what I call an evergreen list.

Master list is the one that I use to broadcast from, like we were talking about on a weekly basis, however often you sit down to write and publish a letter. The evergreen list, in my case, is set up to go out every two weeks with stuff that I know that works.

Now how do I know it works?

Because I used it as broadcast letter, right? The ones that were good, they got response either through money or subscribers, or requests for more information. Those are winners, right? Those got put on a blog so that they're always archived where people can find them, and they also get stuck in this evergreen thing that goes out every two weeks, with the winners forever.

Now I have at least a year of those things queued in there, and at the end of the year, guess what happens? It loops back to the beginning, actually to the second one, because the beginning one is a "welcome to" and I don't want to go back to the "welcome to."

Participant: Does anyone notice the repetition?

Well, let me ask you. Have you noticed? So the answer is no, you haven't noticed nor does anybody else. I mean, that's a year ago, and it loops back a year. Remember how an hour ago, can you remember an hour ago when you told me that we don't remember what we read last week. So how are we going to do a year from now?

Participant: Mark, how do you take one subscriber e-mail and fill it in into three lists? I assume that's because you're not using third-party software?

Mark: Right, but you can actually do this on AWeber, too. Yeah, you can split it into different lists. You can say, "If somebody signs to this list, have them be subscribed to this other list, also." I'll show you how it's done. I will show you inside bypass. How about that?

As a matter of fact, there's three words right there. Properties. So when somebody signs up to this list, see this box that says, "Add to these publications"? They also gets added to, see the master list is marked? And also to the news list. The news list is the thing which goes out every two weeks, and the master list is what I personally publish to whenever I feel like it.

So that's how it is set up.

Now people are sneakier these days, aren't they? They know about using phony e-mail addresses or throwaway e-mail addresses or secondary or tertiary e-mail addresses. So not always does it happen the way you plan.

The more people know you, like you, trust you, the more likely they are to use their real e-mail address, because they do want you to show up in their e-mail box. Okay?

So the longer the relationship you have with them when they start signing up for other reports and the special little goodies that you do, they will start using their real e-mail addresses. Then when they buy they're going to use their primary e-mail addresses 95% of the time, or higher.

The Difference Between A Re-Direct And Cloaked Link

Participant: Mark, what's the difference between a re-direct and cloaked link?

Mark: I don't know. Well, it depends. There are search engine cloaking where you're cloaking pages. You're not talking about that? Okay, there is one way to do it where you're using a frame page, thank you, where you are setting 100% and 0% and you are loading in the sales page into a frame on your site, and it looks like they'd never left your site.

Okay?

That got me banned from Google for a year and a half. There is a whole story to that, too. It wasn't anything dastardly that I was trying to do, this came from all these affiliate links that I had set up back in 1997 or 1998, whenever I started doing this stuff with all the affiliate programs. I had them set up that way so that it looked like nobody ever left my site, right?

Well, because of all the naughty people that do stuff on the Internet and try to trick people as to where they're going, and various sites with different amounts of clothing and such, the search engines frowned upon these kinds of frame set kind of situations. So if you use frame sets, they thought that you were a bad guy.

So apparently I got caught in that net of being assumed to be a bad guy, because I used frames that I had on there for seven years. I don't know, I am not trying to do anything sneaky.

I also noticed that I was not on Google search anymore. You could see me mentioned and links back to me, but if you searched for www.Hunteridge.com it didn't show up at all.

So I'd write to them and never hear back, never hear back, and so finally the third or fourth time I wrote I was getting more upset, and then they finally write me back, and they quoted something in their terms of service that made no sense at all to me. I couldn't figure out what it was.

Then I wrote back and the same thing came back again. Then the third time I wrote back and basically I said, "Look, enough of the games! Will you guys just have somebody check things out and tell me what's wrong and I will be happy to fix it. I am not trying to trick anybody. What's the deal?"

They finally wrote me back and said, "Well..." I didn't understand the answer time, so I gave up and six months go by. So I'd try again.

Anyway, long story short, a year-and-a-half goes by when finally somebody said something about frames, and I am trying to think, "Frames? What am I doing with frames?"

Then it's like, "Ah! These affiliate links!" I went back and I had 50 or 60 of those things, and I had to go back and edit all those and have them fixed. Then I wrote back to them and said, "It's all done, go take a look."

They don't answer, they don't respond, and it's the same cat and mouse game back and forth. You can tell that I love those people.

I kind of gave up and all of a sudden, you know how you pop up a browser sometimes and you start typing before you know what you are doing? Well, somehow Google had popped up and I had typed in Hunteridge.com and I just hit enter without looking. All of a sudden I see a bunch of pages again, and a month ago I guess I was back on Google.

I don't know if I am there now, but all of a sudden it turned back on again. So now I am white hat all over again.

[Laughter]

Okay, so those are the quickest ways to make bucks, is as an affiliate, because you don't have to do a product.

If They Were Better Marketers They Would Go Out And Find People Who Already Want To Buy And Are Willing To Pay

See, it all comes back to, folks, finding people who want to buy something. Why do you think corporations have sales forces? Think about this.

What?

Participant: Sales forces are there to go out and look for the people who want to buy what they're selling.

Mark: Yes, but why, why, why do companies need and hire sales forces?

Participant: Because nobody is going to find them if they don't send somebody out.

Mark: Right. That's because the people who make the products, the people who manage the company, haven't got a clue how to sell stuff!

That's why they need sales people.

Participant: Yeah, that's why they send people out cold-calling door-to-door, which doesn't work.

Mark: Whatever it is, I mean they just beat the bushes and they drag a proverbial dog down the street until somebody says, "Yeah, I want it."

Eventually somebody will say, "Yeah, I'll take it." But that's the shotgun approach that a lot of companies use. Now, if they were better marketers they would go out and find people who already want to buy and are willing to pay.

You've heard me say it how many times today?

If I can get that into your heads and you started believing it, your life will turn around, sales-wise.

This is the story of my life, okay? One-on-one sales.

No, no, no, no, no, no, no, no, no, no, no, yes. All right!

No, no, no, no, no, no, no, no, yes.

You get a lot more no's than yeses; that's sales.

"I've got a hook and you are fish. Can I shove this down your throat?"

That's sales. Whereas with marketing it's, "Are you a fish? Do you like worms? Are you hungry?"

If you answered yes to all three, I'll continue my presentation. If you said no at any point in that interview, I am off to talk to hopefully a different fish.

Do you see the difference?

I don't want to waste my time trying to shove hooks down throats. I want to find gaping hungry mouths ready to clamp on anything that I throw in front of them. That's the marketer mindset.

More Traffic Generation And List Building Tips

"The fastest and least expensive way to generate traffic?"

I gave you almost 30 different ways to do that earlier.

We talked about joint ventures and it says, "JVs are great, but if you're new you have to establish the metrics to attract a JV partner with a decent list."

That's absolutely right, however, remember from talking this morning, a lot of times in joint ventures you have different assets than the metrics. The way to get to know people is to find out what that person wants most, and play to that.

It may not be that they want more money; it may be that they want to have more fun.

I can think of one guy that I know that calls me up, and he is such a stitch that I don't mind taking his telephone calls. But he has taken that slot in my life, so it's okay.

[Laughter]

There is some entertainment value to the phone call, and so I mean it's just that the stuff that comes out is so hilarious, it's like a diversion for me. It kind of gets my mind, my conscious mind, off of things. My subconscious mind can still work and I can talk with him and lighten up and help him out, and at the same time have a few laughs and then I'm back to work. Eventually it's like, "Okay, I've got to get back to work."

"The fastest way and best way to build your list?"

The fastest way is probably some of these giveaway things. By the way, these 12 Days of Christmas, you should be on the hunt for those kind of things.

ISS group, we have a deal that they feed those to me and I disseminate that information out to all the ISS members, so we stay on top of those things.

Those Amazon book runs, where somebody tries to fly an Amazon book up the flagpole and be a number-one seller for the day, those are good things to do.

The things you need to know about doing that if you're going to participate in those, is you've got to have something unique.

If it's a, "Me, too! Me, too!" kind of situation, it's not going to work real well for you.

And everything has to be congruent on the page, where it spotlights your the giveaway gift. When it goes over to your page, it has to have the same kind of look and feel. You don't want people to like walk from room to room and have them think, "Wow! How did I get here? They zapped me across the Internet all of a sudden, and I liked where I was! But when I get over here, this is really weird."

What happens when fish get scared? They swim away.

People are the same way.

"Do you agree with some experts who state that RSS will replace e-mail marketing, or at least should comprise of a large part of how to maintain contact with your prospects?"

I declare that RSS personalized publishing can take the place of commercial e-mail marketing. Personal e-mail will be here to stay, and it's the stuff that will get through the filters.

Just the little short things that you write? There's none of that unsubscribe stuff down at the bottom, there's none of that disclosure that you have to put in as commercial mail. There's no hype words.

Just the stuff that you write to your friends.

By the way, that's why I suggest that you send out personal e-mails. I mean, not personalized, but personal letters without the hype. When I run my e-mails through these things to see how they are going to do on the spam filters, do you know what score I get invariably on these things? Zero, which is good. It means I've got no points against me.

That means I am not using all the hype stuff and I'm not using exclamation points and I am not using capital letters, and not doing this silly little f**e, and all that kind of stuff that people think is fooling the spam filters.

Guess what? They figured that out! I mean, if you can't read it by a human, don't you think it's easy to make a computer read that and see that someone is trying to trick us? Yes.

[Laughter]

So RSS is going to take a big chunk of that, once it becomes to where 80% of the marketplace is using it. Once that Internet Explorer 7 hits, the public doesn't have to know what it is.

Like do you all understand how e-mail works? No, nobody does, right? It just works! I press buttons and stuff shows up on my screen. I type and I press a button and it goes to them.

You don't know how it works, right? You don't know that it's sitting up on some server place and you have to login. All this stuff gets done automatically and it's just there. You just get to use it.

It's become that easy, the technology.

RSS will be there, probably within a year, to where this will all happen, instead of your e-mail reader you may have the RSS readers built into your Internet Explorer 7. Then at that point in, we're going to be able to, instead of having you check your e-mail at your ISP, those stinking spam blockers that filter out good guys, too. We will be able to go directly from publisher directly to your RSS reader.

I see zero spam because the only thing you are going to get in that box is stuff you signed up for. However, that doesn't mean that those kinds of minds can't dream up something.

That's the reason why people like RSS now, is they can pull content off of blogs, or sites, or news, or wherever it is, and have it show up in their reader and personalize the content being shown in the reader.

Nothing else shows up in the reader, and this is the same concept that Bypass had for a couple of years. That was ahead of the curve. Now after it's re-released and Internet 7 is available, that's going to make it all happen.

You see, I'll be able to send you audio and video in them, full graphics and colors and everything. Now the audio and video is actually hosted on my server, but I will be able to link to it. Like the Camtasia video stuff? I will be able to send all the shockwave code to where it will be right in there, and it's going to go pull the video off my server and there it is in your reader.

"Dear Bob, Mark here with the video I think you are going to think is real cool. Just press here."

It's going to show up right there, you don't have to go any place else, it will all be right there.

If you don't want to hear from me, you just take me off your RSS list and that's it.

So is the publisher going to have to get good? Right.

Now they say, "Well, why is that better than just RSS, Mark? Where you'd actually have somebody in your database, and you can sequentially publish to them and broadcast to them and personalize it?"

Well, here is the reason why.

Sales.

Let's go back to sales for a second. Most things are not bought by humans unless they're pushed at a human. Humans have to be made aware that they want things, or excuse me, reminded.

That's where e-mail is so good.

Deliverability is a problem, but e-mail is a reminder service. "We're keeping in touch, you're interested in this, remember? You're interested in this, remember? You want to take action on this, remember? Here are some new things for you, remember?"

Whereas in RSS, the person signs for it and yeah, it shows up there, but it's not necessarily the latest and greatest, it's just news. How much news can you stand in your life? Whereas if it's somebody writing to you in a personal way, it is lot more interesting, isn't it?

Don't you like to open up things to see what it's all about, because you never know what to expect? And it's saying the same-old-same-old.

Okay, I am going to stop with the pre-conference questions there.

Go ahead, go ahead.

Participant: A housekeeping question; what's the schedule for tomorrow? You said one o'clock at one time and six o'clock at another.

Mark: Eight o'clock till six. I am going to go from eight o'clock till six; same kind of schedule.

Rapid Fire Tips And Secrets

Here's something I do on our ISS teleconferences, and I want to do it with y'all, too. You have taken a lot of notes today, some of you?

Take out another piece of paper from the bottom half of one, or wherever it is, and I am going to give you ten seconds to do this. It's the Ten Second Drill.

Think about what I'm about to say.

Is everybody ready?

I want you to write down the three most important things you learned today. The three most important things you learned today.

Put your pen on the paper and start writing.

10, 9, 8, 7, start writing, 6, 5…time's up.

Steve Hamby, do you have a microphone? Now here's what's interesting. Some of the things are going to be the same that you've written down; some of the things are going to be different than you wrote down.

So if you hear something different, write it down.

Okay?

Steve?

Participant: Having a lot of niches is a viable model, and I need to get AdWord, is it miracle or magic?

Mark: AdWord Miracle. I don't know, I don't know. It's www.Hunteridge.com/awm.htm whatever it is. I don't know what it's called. It doesn't matter.

Participant: Are we going around?

Mark: Yep, everybody is going to talk, just quick.

Participant: I got to meet Mark Hendricks and really see how genuine he is. I learned a little bit about some audio software that I didn't know about, and I have confirmed that I wish to be an ISS member.

Mark: Cool. Very good.

Mark: Doesn't matter, we will get everybody; I am not going to leave anybody out.

Participant: Seven tips for $25 or less on how to market an info product, and the ClickBank information.

Mark: Now, if you didn't write these down, jot them down. It will jog your memory, as we have talked about.

Bob?

Participant: How important personalized RSS is going to be, particularly within the year when Internet Explorer 7 comes out. The way you broke down the A, B, and C list and how to contact for JV's with the A people, the B people, the C people. And also the software that you have for the ClickBank affiliate.

Participant: I learned that GPS machines aren't flawless.

[Laughter]

I also learned that eBay.com gets more traffic than Google now; gets more searches than Google now. And I am interested in the CBAccountManager. I didn't know about it and I am going to get home and try it out.

Participant: Well, all I have is know you, like you, trust you, and think I was thinking about dinner.

[Laughter]

Mark: Well, you picked up a good concept, the know you, like you, trust you. If you can get that working for you, a lot of other stuff falls into place because you don't have to be phony. That's really, really important. You can be exactly yourself because see, know you, like you, trust you, plays into the word integrity.

And you can't buy that. Okay?

That's something you prove to the world that you have, and your bright and shining armor can be tarnished very, very quickly by one little slip.

So as you build your integrity and your reputation for integrity, that's something you need to guard with everything you have got, okay?

Good point.

Participant: I liked about writing the twelve articles and making them into chapters for the free giveaway. I think that was a very good idea. The second one would be the CBAccountManager; I liked that. And I liked the audio and video software that you showed, because I really didn't know how to do that either. Thanks.

Mark: All that audio and video stuff, just get the software, wherever you want to start at, whatever level, and just start doing it. Just like you learned to copy and paste in Word documents, and stuff like that, it's exactly the same concept. It's just that they call things a little bit differently, and you have to kind of learn the lingo. In the help sections, just work your way through them and get comfortable, and you will be producing audio and video as good as anybody out there.

It's just the question of getting the content right, but in that kind of stuff there's technology that you've got to learn about before you can get into the game. It's not hard, you just have to have the tenacity to learn it.

Dana?

Participant: On that note, it was the same thing for me, that whole audio and video equipment you went over. I was also intrigued with how I could establish expert status in any niche market and working with experts in that regard.

Mark: And, by the way, who is an expert here?

Participant: And we are all experts and that also was a big revelation, and I appreciated the tips that you gave on communicating with the list of subscribers, the practical tips. And also the importance to write to the emotional appeal and the desires of the people in our copy; and not their logic.

Mark: Okay. Cool.

Participant: I appreciated all the tips and links and leads which take us to so many directions, besides your useful information in the six psychological triggers, and ClickBank, and a lot of stuff. I look forward to tomorrow.

Mark: Make sure that you write down those six psychological triggers on an index card and post them where you can see them next to your computer. Put those in everything you do, in that order, and then notice the other e-mails that you get, especially from me. I consciously try to do it, or at least subconsciously it's there.

Then look at other sales letters and pages and see if you can't spot some of those things. I mean, some are easier to spot, some are used more obviously than others, but I'm telling you that you can, in two or three sentences, you can pack all six of those things in there, and create a really powerful message.

Participant: I learned that you, Mark, are the number one guru on the list. Honesty, no BS thing, that remains and that's comforting, learned the difference between marketing and sales and why I would want to call myself a marketer. And something very disturbing, which is my financial guru is seemingly having problems with his GPS and that kind of scares me.

[Laughter]

Participant: Mark, I learned that your list only needs to be one person to get started; that the product comes last in the process, and to ask them what they want,

Participant: I learned how to create an e-book with the 12 articles, which somebody mentioned earlier. I think that was great. Re-branding the articles; once you get them, you rewrite them. And building lists with squeeze pages.

Participant: I learned about the audio and video software. I thought that was really neat; a lot of which I hadn't heard about before. I really thought the things about the article creation were cool, and how easy it was to put it together and kind of get it rolling and make it go. The other thing was the sales triggers; the psychological triggers that I haven't heard before.

Mark: Over lunch one of gals, I may have been Dana who mentioned this to me, that over past few years she has been learning so many different things, and kind of where she was at, if I can paraphrase a little bit, was that she came to the realization that all the stuff is really easy.

It is.

The problem is you are scattered all over the place, and you are stretched in every direction, and you're having trouble focusing on anything for a given time.

Has anybody ever noticed that, if you have ADD, the Internet is for you! Right?

[Laughter]

It is never ending, and if your attention is quick you can be all over the place. How many windows can you have open at the same time, and all this kind of stuff?

Participant: I learned that it is best to write to your list in a personal letter style, and to work with using emotions to sell, and have actionable content, and use all six of the psychological triggers.

Mark: Yes. Right. It's really powerful. Really powerful.

Participant: I also liked the golf site. The golf site was a really nice model; something really simple to follow through on and repeat. We also liked what you're doing when somebody subscribes, how they end up on three different lists, how they were sequenced and things like that. The RSS e-mailing; I wasn't familiar with that and so that's some food for thought, also.

Mark: Yeah, you will be seeing more of that kind of stuff in probably the next year, offered by lot of people.

Participant: I learned that to know what our customers want, is to ask them through a survey. How to build a list faster is to give something, or to offer something to them. I loved most the ClickBank Account Manager where I want to be an affiliate. Thank you.

Participant: Yeah, there was so much good. For me the most important or the most valuable were the actionable content realization, because I do offer an awful lot of content and it didn't really strike me, until you raised that point that, a lot of it I am just giving away. I am not asking for any action to be taken, so that was a big benefit. Another big benefit is I always at the end of e-books that I write, have as one of the appendices a list of products and/or services that I recommend. It didn't hit me to put at least one of them up at the front of the book, because most people won't make it through. So that was very valuable. And I also very much liked the JV information that you gave me and the competitive grid.

Mark: Yeah, that really works; the competitive grid. You can enter the marketplace standing on everybody else's shoulders. It's a good positioning thing.

Participant: So thank you.

Mark: You're welcome.

Participant: I learned that you can pack a lot into 8:00 to 6:00 today, while you are having fun to boot! [Laughter]

I really liked the AV information, and I can see using that to some really good advantage. I liked the know you, like you, trust you and I am really delighted to have met you finally in person, after being in a few rounds of your 12 Days of Christmas, and going nuts. I really like all the links that you gave us today that are on www.hunteridge.com That was really cool. I'm looking forward to tomorrow's session, even though I have to go back home and unpack boxes.

Mark: Let me ask you, was today of value to you?

Participant: Yes! [Applause]

Mark: And we are looking forward to round two tomorrow?

Okay. All right.

# # # # # # #

To get the audio MP3 recordings of this series, you can visit this website:

http://hunteridge.com/2day

See more books by Mark Hendricks at:

http://amazon.com/author/markhendricks

And visit his main website at:

http://hunteridge.com

# # # # # # #

Legal Notices: Neither the Author or the Publisher assumes any responsibility for errors, inaccuracies or omissions. Any slights of people or organizations are unintentional. If advice concerning tax, legal or related matters is needed, the services of a qualified professional should be sought. This book is not intended for use as a source of legal, accounting or financial advice. Also some suggestions made in this book concerning sales and marketing and business practices may have inadvertently introduced practices deemed unlawful in certain states or municipalities. You should be aware of the various laws governing advertising, sales, marketing and other business practices in your particular industry and in your marketplace.

The Publisher also notes that certain offers of books, tapes, other products and services have been made in this book and reserves the right to modify or withdraw those offers at any time.